Rice Market Liberalization and Poverty in Viet Nam

Nicholas Minot

Francesco Goletti

International Food Policy Research Institute
Washington, D.C.

Library of Congress Cataloging-in-Publication Data

Minot, Nicholas.
Rice market liberalization and poverty in Vietnam / Nicholas Minot, Francesco Goletti.
p. cm—(Research report ; 114)
Includes bibliographical references.
ISBN 0-89629-117-0
1. Rice trade—Vietnam. 2. Poor—Vietnam.
3. Vietnam—Economic conditions—20th century.
4. Vietnam—Economic policy. I Goletti, Francesco.
II. Title. III. Research report (International Food Policy Research Institute) ; 114

HD9066.V52 M56 2001
381′.41318′09597—dc21 00-050574

Contents

Tables

Figures

Foreword

Agricultural market liberalization has been the subject of numerous studies by IFPRI and other research organizations. Recent and forthcoming IFPRI research reports on this topic include studies of maize marketing in the Philippines by Meyra Mendoza and Mark Rosegrant, of the ASEAN Free Trade Agreement by Dean DeRosa, of groundnut market liberalization in Senegal by Ousmane Badiane et al., and of Egyptian wheat market reforms by Mylène Kherallah et al.

The case of rice market liberalization in Viet Nam is interesting and distinctive in three ways. First, Viet Nam is in the midst of a transition from a centrally planned economy to a market-oriented one. The very success of this process in stimulating economic growth and rice exports created a situation in which policymakers and researchers had only a partial picture of the newly transformed rice marketing system.

Second, rice is both the most important export crop in Viet Nam and the dominant staple food. The dual role of rice in the economy created an apparent contradiction between food security objectives and the desire to promote exports. The political sensitivity of rice export policy is heightened by the memory of rice exports in the first half of the 20th century that coincided with periods of deprivation and even famine.

Third, Viet Nam's agroclimatic diversity and long distances imply that the effects of rice policy will vary widely by region. This diversity further complicates the task of anticipating the effect of changes in rice policy on poor and vulnerable households.

In this study, Nicholas Minot and Francesco Goletti examine the new patterns of rice marketing in Viet Nam and study how liberalizing both internal and external rice markets has affected food security and poverty. For the first task, they make use of a comprehensive set of surveys carried out by IFPRI in 1995–96. These surveys, covering rice producers, traders, millers, and state-owned enterprises, provide a detailed picture of the new rice marketing system in Viet Nam.

For the second task, they assess the household-level impact of rice policy by combining a spatial equilibrium model with household survey data. The spatial equilibrium model is used to simulate the effect of rice policy on food markets in seven agroclimatic regions of Viet Nam. The survey data are then used to estimate the impact of simulated price changes in each region on real income and poverty among different groups of households.

The results suggest that export liberalization does raise rice prices within the country, but that the effects are smaller (in percentage terms) as one moves away from the rice export zone. Furthermore, the higher prices have a positive effect on rural income and a mixed but slightly favorable impact on poverty. Furthermore, relaxing restrictions on the internal movement of rice from south to north also generates net benefits for the country without increasing poverty.

The results of the analysis in this report were presented to Vietnamese policymakers in late 1996, leading them to enact a series of annual increases in the rice export quota and to lift restrictions on internal rice trade. In the wake of these reforms, rice prices have been stable or declined and the north-south price margin has narrowed, showing that sound policy research can lead to beneficial policy actions.

It is important to stress that the specific findings of this study are not necessarily applicable to other countries that export a staple food crop. Under different circumstances, policymakers may face a more serious trade-off between exports and rural poverty. The study does, however, indicate that the effects of market reform on poverty are not always intuitive. More important, it provides a methodological tool for examining the impact of agricultural trade and marketing policy on poor households in developing countries.

Per Pinstrup-Andersen
Director General

Acknowledgments

The authors gratefully acknowledge financial support from the Asian Development Bank for funding the Rice Market Monitoring and Policy Options Project (TA No. 222-VIE), upon which this report is based. Additional financial support for the project was provided by the International Food Policy Research Institute (IFPRI).

The work would not have been possible without the help of many people in Viet Nam. We are particularly grateful to the Department of Planning and Projection (DPP) of the Ministry of Agriculture and Rural Development (MARD), whose former director, Dr. Huynh Xuan Hoang, was our main counterpart during the implementation of the project. He provided support and helped in converting our findings into policy formulation for the government. The day-to-day liaison with the ministry was provided by Dr. Do Dinh Thuan, vice director of the DPP. The Department of Agricultural and Rural Development Policy and its former director, Dr. Cao Duc Phat (currently vice minister of MARD), were also instrumental in bringing the results of the study into the policy debate. The continuous support of Dr. Prof. Ngo The Dan, senior vice minister of MARD, helped us clarify some of the key policy issues and provided policy commitment to the type of research we were undertaking.

Various people helped us in the collection of data from the field all over Viet Nam. Teams of field workers stayed in the field for several months between December 1995 and June 1996 and were key to collecting one of the most comprehensive databases on rice production and marketing in Viet Nam. We want to acknowledge the supervision and research collaboration of Dr. Nguyen The Binh, vice director of the National Institute for Planning and Projection (NIAPP), and Mr. Nguyen Van Tung, currently at the Government Office.

Mr. Hoang Trung Lap of NIAPP managed the data entry, and the indefatigable Mr. Nguyen Viet Hai of the Department of Science and Technology and Product Quality of MARD helped us solve so many daily difficulties that without him, we would not have been able to complete the study within the time allowed.

Numerous people have also contributed to this study by sharing their experience, time, and information, including officials from various government agencies (including the Ministry of Planning and Investment and the Government Price Committee), members of local People's Committees, researchers from several organizations (Hanoi Agricultural University, Can Tho University, the Rice Research Institute, and the Viet Nam Agricultural Science Institute), and the thousands of farmers, traders, millers, and enterprises involved in rice sector. To all of them, we express our most sincere appreciation.

We would also like to thank our colleagues at IFPRI: Philippe Berry for his extensive involvement in the field work and data analysis, Lisa Grover and Diana Flores for their professional editing work, and Raisuddin Ahmed for constant encouragement. Finally, the report benefited significantly from useful comments and suggestions provided by Emmanuel Eskoufias of IFPRI and by two anonymous external reviewers.

Summary

This report focuses on market liberalization in the rice sector of Viet Nam and its impact on income and poverty. This topic is of interest for several reasons. First, the transition from central planning to a market-oriented economy in Viet Nam has been more extensive and more rapid than in many other nations. Second, on an aggregate level, the reform of the rice sector has been successful in transforming the country from a rice importer to a major exporter. Third, rice policy is important to the 76 million inhabitants of Viet Nam because rice accounts for three-quarters of the caloric intake and is grown by more than two-thirds of Vietnamese households. And finally, since Viet Nam now supplies 9 to 17 percent of world exports, the prospects for exports have important implications for world rice markets.

The main objective of this report is to examine the new set of food policy issues facing Viet Nam as a result of its transformation into a major rice exporter and its transition toward a market economy. In particular, the report aims to shed some light on two key issues: (1) What would be the effect on income and poverty of further liberalization of rice markets in Viet Nam? (2) What lessons can other countries learn from market liberalization in Viet Nam?

The liberalization of Vietnamese agriculture has proceeded in a series of small steps in response to poor agricultural performance and reduced assistance from the Soviet Union. Reforms began in 1980 with the introduction of the contract system, accelerated in 1988 with the devolution of decisionmaking to the farm household, and were complemented by liberalization of other sectors in the early 1990s. These reforms have generated impressive results, with rice production and the agricultural sector growing at close to 5 percent per year.

Rice production in Viet Nam is characterized by small irrigated farms, multiple cropping, labor-intensive practices, and growing use of inorganic fertilizer, though there are substantial regional differences. The Mekong River Delta is the rice bowl of Viet Nam, producing about half of national output on relatively "large" farms of 1.1 hectare. The Red River Delta is one of the most densely populated agricultural areas in the world. Although farms average only 0.25 hectares, the Red River Delta manages to produce rice surpluses, though they are much smaller than those of the

Mekong. Rice cultivation is less intensive in the other regions, but rice is by far the most important staple in every region.

More than 57 percent of the rice production growth during 1985–95 was accounted for by yield growth, with rice area actually declining. Crop intensification (increasing the number of crops per year) and interaction among these factors accounts for the rest. Although all regions have seen impressive rice production growth, the Mekong Delta accounts for two-thirds of national growth.

There is little potential for expansion of rice area and only minimal potential for further intensification. Rice output growth will increasingly rely on yield expansion. Yield growth has far exceeded the Asian average, probably reflecting lagged response to liberalization. Thus, yield growth can be expected to fall in the coming years.

The structure of the rice marketing system in Viet Nam suggests that it has rapidly developed into a complex system without the central management that policymakers once thought was necessary. Tens of thousands of traders handle millions of tons of rice every year, channeling it from surplus farmers to urban consumers, rural rice-deficit areas, and exporters. Furthermore, the channels are numerous and differ from one region to another. The role played by the state-owned enterprises in the rice marketing system is minimal, except in the area of long-distance trade, where it dominates, and exports, where it has a legal monopoly.

As the overall economy has stabilized, rice prices have become less volatile, but market liberalization does not seem to have had a noticeable effect on marketing margins between paddy and rice prices, between farm and retail prices, or between prices in the north and south of the country. Spatial market integration analysis indicates that the degree of market integration has increased somewhat since the late 1980s, but it remains weak.

Two types of restrictions on trade affect the performance of the marketing system. First, internal trade was restricted in 1995, as indicated by the responses of traders in a 1995–96 IFPRI survey and by the large price differential between rice prices in the north and south. Second, the rice export quota is used by the government to ensure adequate domestic supplies. This report compares domestic and border prices, finding that the rice export quota was binding at least over the period 1990–95 and that it was equivalent to an export tax of 20 to 25 percent.

Rice is by far the most important staple in the Vietnamese diet, accounting for more than 60 percent of the caloric intake in every region. Per capita rice consumption is lower among urban households than rural ones. In addition, rice consumption rises with income at low and middle income levels, but it falls as income rises further. Econometric analysis of household data carried out in this study suggests that the expenditure elasticity of rice demand is 0.38 at the mean income level, while the price elasticity is −0.24.

In order to understand how a rice policy affects the poor, the distribution of poverty in Viet Nam is examined. Poverty is almost four times as widespread and five times as severe in the rural areas as in the urban areas. Furthermore, poverty tends to be concentrated in the more remote, hilly regions, namely the North Central Coast, the

Northern Uplands, and the Central Highlands. Household survey data suggest that the two delta regions, with 45 percent of the population, are surplus regions that would gain from higher rice prices; the other five regions are rice-deficit areas that would lose on average. Higher prices would also benefit the average rural household at the expense of urban households.

A uniform 10 percent increase in rice prices would hurt urban households, nonfarmers, and residents of the five deficit regions, although the effect on real income would be less than 2 percent on average. On average, the price increase would benefit farmers, particularly those in the Red River and Mekong deltas. Somewhat paradoxically, in spite of the higher average income, the poverty rate would rise slightly from 25.0 to 25.2 percent in the long run.

A simulation model, the Viet Nam Agricultural Spatial Equilibrium Model, was constructed to examine the impact of alternative rice marketing policies on prices, production, consumption, and income. The impact on poverty is estimated by combining the results of the simulations with household data on rice marketing patterns.

With regard to the rice export quota, the model indicates that there is some justification for the concern of the Vietnamese government that eliminating rice export quotas would raise prices and hurt some Vietnamese households. The model confirms that rice prices would rise 14 to 22 percent (depending on whether internal restrictions were also removed) and have an adverse effect on urban households, nonfarm rural households, and households in the Central Highlands. For example, according to the 1992–93 Viet Nam Living Standards Survey, the poorest quintile of urban households spends almost one-third of their income on rice.

At the same time, the model shows that the net gains to rice farmers and consumers would be around US$200 million. Three-quarters of this gain would represent a transfer from state-owned enterprises exporting rice and one-quarter a net gain to the country. Furthermore, poor households tend to gain both in absolute terms and relative to nonpoor households because they are predominantly rural farmers who benefit from higher rice prices.

The government could liberalize rice exports slowly by replacing the quota with an export tax and gradually reducing the tax rate. The model indicates that a 22 percent tax would be equivalent to the 2.5 million tons quota. This option has the advantage of generating revenue that could be used to alleviate the impact of higher rice prices through targeted assistance.

With regard to restrictions on the internal movement of food, the model suggests that the impact on *average* prices and incomes would be relatively small. Nonetheless, the absolute gains are large compared with the negligible costs of such a policy. Removing restrictions on internal trade would have substantial regional effects, however, lowering prices in the north and raising them in the south. The distributional effects are relatively small and tend to cancel each other, so there is no change in the national poverty rate.

CHAPTER 1

Introduction

Over the past 20 years, market liberalization has been a dominant feature of economic reforms in developing countries. In the early 1980s, the adoption of more market-oriented policies was an important component of the structural adjustment programs adopted by developing countries. This trend has been extended to a new set of countries since 1989 with the dissolution of the Soviet Union and the eastern bloc.

The process of market liberalization, however, has not been free of controversy. Perhaps the most common criticism is that market liberalization is said to have had adverse effects on the poor through layoffs in formerly-state-owned industries, higher food prices, and the erosion of social safety net programs (Cornia, Jolly, and Jolly 1987).

Higher food prices may result from price deregulation, removal of subsidies, depreciation of an overvalued exchange rate, relaxation of compulsory government procurement policies, or removal of export controls. Higher food prices almost certainly have a negative impact on the urban poor, since they spend a relatively large share of their budgets on food. But the effect of higher food prices on the rural poor is ambiguous because they are both producers and consumers of staple foods.

The impact of food prices on the welfare of the poor has been the topic of numerous studies. Mellor (1978) noted that the direct welfare effect of higher food prices depends on the net sales position of the household: net sellers, such as commercial farmers, gain, while net buyers, such as urban consumers and landless rural households, lose. Other studies show a surprisingly high proportion of net food buyers among rural households in developing countries (Weber et al.1988; Sahn 1988; and Barrett and Dorosh 1996). Deaton (1989) combines household data and hypothesized price changes to study the distributional effect of higher rice prices that would result from export liberalization in Thailand. Similar methods were adopted in studies of the distributional effect of higher food prices in Côte d'Ivoire (Budd 1993) and in Madagascar (Barrett and Dorosh 1996).

Computable general equilibrium models have been widely used to examine the impact of policy on different household groups (for example, see Bourguignon, de Melo, and Morrison 1991). These models are able to simulate the indirect effects of policy via changes in labor markets, land prices, or feedback from nonagricultural sectors. The distributional analysis in these models is, however, usually limited to four to eight household types.

This report focuses on market liberalization in the rice sector of Viet Nam and its impact on poverty. The topic is of interest for several reasons. First, as a country in transition from central planning to a market-oriented economy, the process of liberalization has been more extensive and more rapid than in many other nations. Second, on an aggregate level, the reform of the rice sector has been successful in transforming the country from a rice importer to a major exporter. Third, the importance of rice policy to the 76 million inhabitants of Viet Nam is evident from the fact that rice accounts for three-quarters of the caloric intake and is grown by more than two-thirds of Vietnamese households. And finally, since Viet Nam now supplies 9 to 17 percent of world rice exports, Vietnamese rice policy and the prospects for exports have important implications for world rice markets. The next section provides some background on the importance of rice in Viet Nam and the evolution of rice policy.

Rice in Viet Nam

Rice has played a central role in the lives of the people of Viet Nam for several thousand years. The Chinese and Vietnamese kingdoms that ruled the region are judged by historians, and presumably by their subjects, by their ability to ensure a steady supply of rice to the population. Prosperous periods, such as the early years of the Ly Dynasty (1009–1225), were noted for their investments in irrigation and dike construction, while the decline of kingdoms was often presaged by the collapse of irrigation systems, leading to food shortages and unrest (Vien 1993).

Large-scale rice exports began in the early 20th century with the installation of large irrigation works in the Mekong Delta under French colonial authority. Tenant farmers in the Mekong produced surpluses, allowing Viet Nam to export 1 to 2 million tons in the 1920s and early 1930s. Under Japanese occupation during World War II, Viet Nam was obligated to supply Japan with 0.9 to 1.0 million tons of rice per year. These exports coexisted with periods of extreme deprivation and hardship, culminating in a famine in 1945–46 in which as many as 600,000 may have perished (Vien 1993, 227). This experience helps explain the sensitivity of policymakers today to the food security implications of rice exports.

Rice continues to play a central role in Vietnamese agricultural production and food consumption. Paddy is grown on 53 percent of the agricultural land in Viet Nam, and it represents 64 percent of the sown area of crops.[1] Rice has recently become the second largest export, accounting for more than 10 percent of the total value. According to the 1992–93 Viet Nam Living Standards Survey (VLSS), 69.9 percent of

[1] The term "paddy" in this report refers to unmilled rice, although technically unmilled upland rice is not considered paddy.

Vietnamese households grow rice and 99.9 percent consume rice.[2] As already mentioned, rice accounts for three-quarters of the caloric intake of the average Vietnamese household.

Thus, it is not surprising that the performance of the rice sector continues to be an important criterion by which the Vietnamese judge government policy. The stagnation of rice production and food shortages in the first decade after unification (1976–86) were perhaps the most important catalyst for questioning the superiority of socialist forms of production. Under the *doi moi* (renovation) policy announced in December 1986, the government began to give markets a greater role in the allocation of resources in the economy. The first reforms were implemented in 1988 in the agricultural sector, decentralizing responsibility for agricultural management from collectives to farm households. These reforms were followed by other measures to stimulate exports, encourage savings, and open the country to foreign investment.

The success of these reforms in the rice sector were dramatic: within a few years, Viet Nam had transformed itself from a chronic rice importer to one of the three largest rice exporters in the world. The dramatic success of the reforms in stimulating rice production and exports made it easier for pro-reform elements in the government to push for market-oriented reforms in other sectors (see Pingali and Xuan 1992).

Rice policy continues to be the subject of intense debate in Viet Nam, as it is in many Asian countries (Sicular 1989). Policymakers give high priority to ensuring adequate incomes for rice farmers and sufficient supply of affordable rice to consumers. The policy issues facing Viet Nam have changed as a result of its new status as a major rice exporter. Although the food shortages that plagued the country in the 1980s have receded, the government faces new trade-offs between generating foreign exchange from rice exports and maintaining low prices for domestic consumers.

In spite of the relaxation of government control over rice production and marketing, until recently important restrictions on rice exports and internal rice trade have been in place. The most important of these restrictions are a binding export quota on rice and various restrictions on rice trade between regions. In addition, state-owned enterprises continue to enjoy a legal monopoly on rice exports. In part, these restrictions reflect a desire to maintain adequate supplies for domestic rice consumers, particularly the poor. The restrictions also reflect a residual suspicion of private traders and doubts regarding the ability of the market to serve the needs of producers and consumers. Finally, there is a fiscal incentive to maintain the current system since the rice-exporting state-owned enterprises contribute part of their profits to the government.

As discussed later, however, it is likely that Viet Nam will be required to liberalize rice export policy when it joins the World Trade Organization. Thus, it is impor-

---

[2] The VLSS was carried out by the State Planning Committee and the General Statistical Office, with support from the World Bank, the United Nations Development Programme, and the Swedish International Development Agency.

tant to understand the impact of alternative rice liberalization policies on income, prices, and poverty.

Objectives

The main objective of this report is to examine the new set of food policy issues facing Viet Nam as a result of its transformation into a major rice exporter and its transition toward a market economy. In particular, the reports aims to shed light on two key questions:

1. What would be the effect on income and poverty of further liberalization of rice markets in Viet Nam?
2. What lessons for other countries can be learned from market liberalization in Viet Nam?

The achievement of this objective can be organized into three tasks. First, the report aims to describe the patterns of rice production and marketing in Viet Nam. The rice marketing system has evolved rapidly in recent years, responding to both substantial increases in marketed surplus and liberalization of marketing policy. The new patterns of rice production and marketing have important implications for the impact of policy on household welfare.

Second, the report attempts to assess the performance of the rice marketing system in Viet Nam. This is accomplished by examining marketing costs, the movement of prices in different markets at the same time, and the relationship between price differences across markets and transportation costs between them. Particular attention is paid to differences in market performance across regions and between private traders and state-owned enterprises (SOEs).

Third, the report examines the impact of alternative rice marketing policies on prices, incomes, production, and consumption in different regions and for different groups of the population.

Methodology

A variety of methods is used to address the various research tasks. The methods combine descriptive analysis, time-series analysis, and economic modeling to draw policy conclusions. Time series methods are used to study trends and variability of the main variables of interest, such as prices and production. Time series models are also used in the study of market integration. Finally, a multimarket spatial equilibrium model of Vietnamese food markets is the main tool used to conduct a series of policy experiments. Each method will be further explained in the following chapters.

The database used in this study combines secondary and primary data. Secondary data such as prices, production, trade, and macroeconomic indicators were obtained from Viet Nam's General Statistical Office, Ministry of Agriculture and Rural Development, and Ministry of Trade. Primary data collection was geared to obtain marketing information that is not available from secondary sources. Four categories of market participants were interviewed: farmers, traders, millers, and SOEs.

The sample selection was designed to represent the rice marketing system of all seven regions of Viet Nam. The sample was stratified by region, and for each region, several provinces were selected in order to capture various characteristics such as the importance of rice production and marketing, remoteness from main markets, closeness to border trade, and agricultural diversification out of rice. Seventeen provinces were selected and, within each province, at least two districts were identified. The sample includes 1,388 farmers, 850 traders, 852 millers, and 36 SOEs. Traders, millers, and SOEs were interviewed in two rounds to capture seasonality. The first round took place between November 1995 and February 1996, while the second round took place between March and June 1996.

Organization

Chapter 2 examines the patterns of rice production and the policy context in Viet Nam. It provides some historical background, studies the sources of growth in rice production since 1985, and summarizes the seasonal and geographic patterns in Vietnamese rice production.

Chapter 3 studies the structure and performance of the rice marketing system in Viet Nam. It uses the IFPRI survey of traders and millers to describe the marketing channels by which rice moves from the farm to domestic consumers and exporters. The chapter also provides several measures of the performance of the Vietnamese rice marketing system.

Chapter 4 looks at the patterns of rice demand in Viet Nam. In addition to descriptive statistics on rice consumption behavior, an econometric model of food demand is presented. This information is used to make simple projections of the trends in rice demand over the coming decades, an issue with important implications for the sustainability of Vietnamese rice exports.

Chapter 5 focuses on the effects of rice price changes on income distribution and poverty. Household survey data are used to estimate which groups would gain and which would lose from higher rice prices.

Chapter 6 uses the spatial equilibrium model to simulate the effect of rice market policy options on income, prices, production, and consumption in each region. Among the policy options considered are relaxation of the export quota, replacing the quota with export taxes, and removing restrictions on the internal movement of rice.

And Chapter 7 summarizes the results of the study, drawing conclusions with regard to rice policy, constraints on the domestic and export market for Vietnamese rice, and prospects for the future. In addition, recommendations are made with regard to methods for studying the impact of marketing policy in other countries.

CHAPTER 2

Rice Production and Policy Context

In the 10 years following the introduction of the *doi moi* policy (renovation), paddy production in Viet Nam increased from about 16 million metric tons in 1986 to over 26 million metric tons in 1996.[3] Examining the factors behind this growth is important both for understanding the transformation of the rice economy in Viet Nam and for evaluating the potential for further expansion. The first section of this chapter provides some background by reviewing the evolution of agricultural policy since 1975 when Viet Nam was reunified. Next, the characteristics of rice production in different parts of the country are described. Third, growth in rice production is decomposed by region and by area, yield, and cropping intensity in order to shed some light on this transformation. The last section addresses the question of the potential for further expansion in rice production in Viet Nam.

Evolution of Agricultural Policy

With the reunification of north and south Viet Nam in 1975, the government faced the challenges of rebuilding from the war and extending the system of agricultural collectives and state-managed industry to the south. With a unified and independent country at peace for the first time in decades, expectations were high. The first five-year plan (1976–80), however, was a failure: none of the 15 production targets was met (Kim 1996, 203). Food production, widely used in Viet Nam as a measure of general welfare, was 31 percent below target and actually fell in per capita terms. Formerly independent farmers in the Mekong Delta resisted cooperativization, and in the north, there was growing recognition that the centralization of cooperative management was eroding farmer incentives. In response, the government promulgated Directive 100 in 1981 under which cooperatives would contract farm households to produce a given amount on their own plots, but any surplus could be sold on the newly liberalized free market (Xuan 1995, 188). Farmers responded well to the new

[3] For the purposes of this report, all tons are metric tons.

incentives: per capita food production grew from 273 kilograms in 1981 to 304 kilograms in 1985, achieving 96 percent of the 1985 target.

In 1985–86, the fiscal deficit balooned as a result of the reduction in assistance by the Soviet Union and the losses of SOEs. Rice production stagnated as hyperinflation eroded the real value of official rice prices, and rising production quotas further reduced farmer incentives. In 1986, the government announced its intention to move toward a more market-oriented economy, a policy known as *doi moi* (renovation). The first concrete manifestation of this policy was Resolution 10 of 1988, which recognized the farm household as the basic unit of agricultural production. Farmers were allowed to buy, own, and sell agricultural inputs such as machines, buffaloes, and tools. Cooperative land was assigned to farming households for 10 to 15 years under different forms of contracts or bidding. Furthermore, farmers were allowed to market 40 percent of contracted output. By 1989, compulsory government purchase of farm products was eliminated, and private traders were allowed to purchase directly from farmers (Pingali and Xuan 1992).

The results were dramatic: rice production grew 57 percent during 1985–95 or 4.6 percent per year; food production per capita increased from 307 kilograms of paddy equivalent in 1988 to 349 kilograms in 1992 and to 372 kilograms in 1995; and agricultural output grew at an annual rate of 5.1 percent between 1988 and 1995. Stimulated by surpluses and more favorable exchange rates, Viet Nam began exporting rice in 1989, rapidly becoming the third largest exporter in the world after Thailand and the United States. In 1997, Vietnamese rice exports surpassed those of the United States, making it the second largest in the world.

Market-oriented reforms were carried out in other sectors as well. The government eliminated most direct subsidies and price controls, tightened government spending, set interest rates positive in real terms, unified and devalued the foreign exchange rate, and moved toward a more liberalized international trade. The government reduced subsidies to SOEs and exposed them to greater competition. As will be discussed later, however, SOEs continue to dominate certain sectors of the economy (Plummer 1995; Irwin 1995; and Doanh and McCarty 1995). Furthermore, although trade restrictions have been greatly reduced, the government limits trade through a variety of administrative controls in a number of key sectors such as rice, fertilizer, and sugar (see CIE 1998; Anderson 1998; and CIE 1999).

Characteristics of Rice Production

Rice production in Viet Nam is characterized by multiple cropping, small irrigated farms, labor-intensive practices, and widespread use of fertilizer. This section briefly describes the pattern of rice production. Although there is considerable regional variation, this report focuses on production systems in the Mekong and Red River deltas, where two-thirds of Vietnamese rice is grown.

Geographic Distribution of Rice Production

Although Viet Nam is a major rice producer, only a small proportion of its territory is suitable for rice cultivation. Less than a quarter of the surface of Viet Nam is agricultural land, most of the remainder consisting of mountainous areas. Of the agricultural land in Viet Nam, however, over half is dedicated to rice production (Table 1).

The Vietnamese compare their country to a *đòn gánh,* a pair of baskets suspended from a pole. The two rice baskets of Viet Nam are the Red River Delta in the north and the Mekong River Delta in the south, connected by a relatively narrow strip of land (see Figure 1). Although the two deltas represent barely 15 percent of the national territory, they account for more than two-thirds of national rice production.

The Red River Delta is the cradle of the Vietnamese culture. Wet rice cultivation was established there as early as 2000 BC, and by 600 BC inhabitants of the Delta were irrigating rice fields using the tidal motion of the rivers and a complex system of dikes and canals (Bray 1986; Cosslett and Shaw 1987). Today it is one of the most densely populated agricultural regions in the world, with more than 1,000 inhabitants per square kilometer, even after excluding Hanoi. The farms are quite small (averaging 0.25 hectare) and intensely cultivated (the cropping intensity ratio for rice is 1.8). Rice is grown by 95 percent of the rural households and accounts for 81 percent of agricultural land. The Red River Delta represents 18 percent of national rice production and produces a surplus of several hundred thousand tons for shipment to surrounding regions (see Table 1).

In contrast to the Red River Delta, large-scale rice cultivation in the Mekong River Delta is a relatively recent phenomenon. At the turn of the century, the French colonial authorities embarked on a large canal-building project to develop the region for rice production (Vien 1993,166). This is reflected today in the lower population density (401 inhabitants per square kilometer), larger farms (1.26 hectares), and a lower cropping intensity. Because it is much larger than the Red River Delta, the Mekong accounts for more than half of Vietnamese rice production. Between 1995 and 1998 it generated a rice surplus ranging between 4.5 and 6 million tons per year, most of which is exported while the remainder is shipped to other regions of the country.

The rest of Viet Nam is divided into five regions. In these regions, a large majority of rural households grow rice, but the yields and cropping intensities are lower than in the two deltas. As a result, all five are rice-deficit regions. The Northern Uplands is a cool, hilly region bordering China on the north and Laos on the west. It is one of the poorest regions, and ethnic minorities represent a large share of the population. Irrigated rice is grown in the narrow mountain valleys and upland rice on the slopes, but the average yields and cropping intensities are low. Livestock (particularly pig production), cassava, and maize are important.

The North Central Coast consists of a narrow coastal plain and a chain of rugged mountains. The coast is more developed and features irrigated rice in the river valleys, but the interior region is poor and sparsely populated. The South Central Coast is similar, but somewhat more developed and has a sizable fishing industry. The Central Highlands is a poor, sparsely populated region with very little commercial rice

Table 1—Area, yield, and production of paddy in 1995

Region	Total area	Agricultural land		Cultivated rice area		Cropping intensity	Sown paddy area	Paddy yield	Paddy production	
		Area	Percent	Area	Percent				Yield	Percent
	(1,000 hectares)	(1,000 hectares)	(of total area)	(1,000 hectares)	(of agri-cultural land)	(ratio)	(1,000 hectares)	(tons/ hectare)	(1,000 tons)	(of national output)
North Uplands	10,297	1,741	16.9	578	33.2	1.40	808	2.79	2,254	9.0
Red River Delta	1,258	712	56.6	578	81.2	1.80	1,042	4.44	4,623	18.5
North Central Coast	5,118	670	13.1	414	61.8	1.65	682	3.14	2,141	8.6
South Central Coast	4,518	545	12.1	273	50.1	1.90	518	3.38	1,749	7.0
Central Highlands	5,618	629	11.2	131	20.8	1.32	173	2.48	430	1.7
Southeast	2,339	956	40.9	278	29.1	1.27	352	2.66	935	3.7
Mekong River Delta	3,956	2,654	67.1	1,951	73.5	1.64	3,191	4.02	12,832	51.4
Viet Nam	33,104	7,907	23.9	4,203	53.2	1.61	6,766	3.69	24,964	100.0

Source: GSO 1996b, 14–15, 18–19, 62–67.

Figure 1—Agroecological regions of Viet Nam

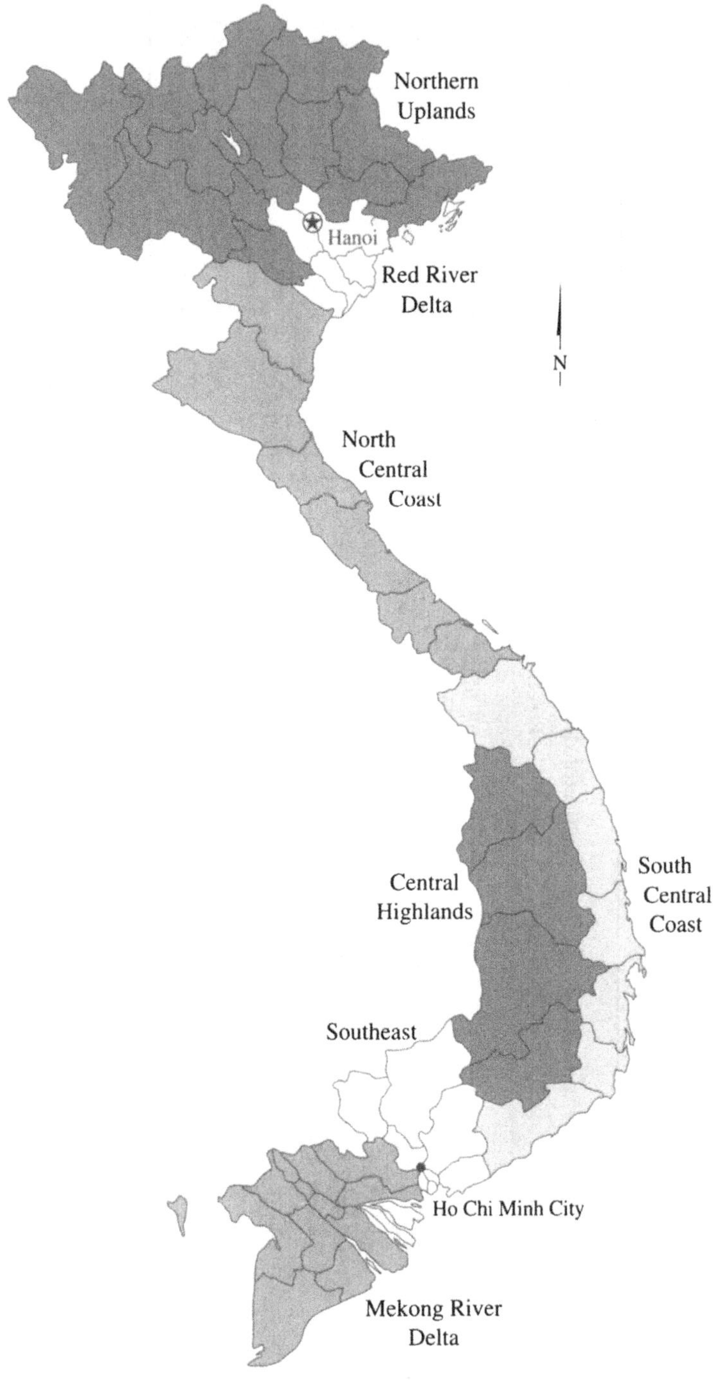

production. Recently, the region has seen a boom in coffee production and a flow of immigrants from other regions. The Southeast region includes Ho Chi Minh City, making it the most urbanized and developed region. Agriculture in the Southeast is less specialized in rice and includes fruit and vegetable production for the urban market and for export, as well as a variety of agribusiness activities such as sugar, starch, feed, and rubber.

Cropping Systems

The average rice cropping intensity in Viet Nam is 1.6, according to the General Statistical Office (GSO). The Agricultural Census of 1994 reports that out of total paddy area, 8.8 percent was triple cropped, 55.2 percent double cropped, and 36 percent single cropped (see GSO 1995b, Vol. 1, 55).[4]

Single-cropped rice includes both upland rice and lowland rainfed rice. Upland rice is unirrigated and is planted on slopes where it is not possible to flood the fields. It is mainly grown in the Central Highlands and the Northern Uplands, generally by ethnic minorities. Often upland rice fields are burned, planted with rice for 2 to 3 years, and then left fallow for 8 to 20 years. The area planted with upland rice in 1993 was estimated at 450,000 hectares in 1993, or 6 percent of the total sown area of rice, though the area affected by this practice is at least 10 times larger. Upland rice area is declining (Arraudeau and Xuan 1995).

Lowland rainfed rice is also unirrigated, but it is planted where rainfall and topography allow the rice fields to be submerged during at least part of the growing season. A significant portion of the Mekong River Delta (600,000 hectares) is rainfed, particularly along the eastern coast and southern Ca Mau peninsula. Rice yields are 2 to 3 tons per hectare. Lowland rainfed rice area is also declining as the irrigation and drainage networks expand (Xuan et al. 1995).

Double cropping of rice is widespread in the Red River Delta, the river basins along the central coast, and the Mekong River Delta. Double cropping may involve one rainy season harvest and one winter-spring harvest. In the Red River Delta, the winter-spring crop is planted in February and harvested in May-June, while in the Mekong this season occurs three months earlier. Alternatively, in the Mekong Delta and other irrigated regions in the south, a double rice rotation may involve a rainy season crop and a summer-autumn rice crop (planted in April-May and harvested in August-September).

In fact, the concept of crop seasons is somewhat artificial since rice is harvested somewhere in Viet Nam every month of the year. As shown in Table 2, March is the month with the largest harvest (about 22 percent of the total), and the four months from May to August contribute an additional 46 percent of total production. Using 1995 production and an assumed consumption of 156 kilograms per capita, the rice deficit can be estimated on a monthly basis, shown in the last column of Table 2. The

---

[4] Farm surveys suggest that triple rice cropping is practiced on about 5 percent of the rice land (Sub-NIAPP 1995), implying that double-cropped rice accounts for 51 percent and single-cropped rice 44 percent.

Table 2—Seasonal distribution of production by region

Month	Northern Uplands	Red River Delta	North Central Coast	South Central Coast	Central High-lands	South-east	Mekong River Delta	Viet Nam	National rice gap
	(percent of annual production)								(1,000 metric tons)
January	0.0	0.0	0.0	0.0	0.0	0.0	3.4	1.8	-715
February	0.0	0.0	0.0	18.3	0.0	0.0	11.6	7.3	46
March	0.0	0.0	0.0	28.8	16.3	24.6	36.0	21.7	2,051
April	0.0	0.0	6.6	8.0	17.0	7.3	7.3	5.4	-206
May	23.3	26.2	46.9	2.7	11.9	0.0	2.4	12.6	793
June	22.2	27.6	0.0	19.0	0.0	3.2	4.0	10.6	514
July	2.3	0.2	0.0	15.8	0.0	23.4	21.7	13.4	898
August	0.0	0.0	33.4	3.4	2.4	27.3	12.2	10.4	489
September	8.6	4.4	13.2	3.1	26.0	6.7	0.6	3.9	-414
October	25.1	35.0	0.0	0.8	12.4	0.0	0.0	9.0	292
November	18.5	6.6	0.0	0.0	6.4	6.4	0.8	3.6	-455
December	0.0	0.0	0.0	0.0	7.7	1.1	0.0	0.2	-935
Total	100.0	100.0	100.0	100.0	100.0	100.0	100.0	100.0	2,357

Source: IFPRI 1996.

Note: The national rice gap refers to the gap between monthly production and monthly consumption, assuming consumption of 156 kilograms per person per year.

month of March generates a surplus of about 2 million tons, while the months of November to January are the lean months. The largest deficit (935,000 tons in December) can be interpreted as the minimum intrayear rice storage requirement consistent with food security.

Farm Size

Vietnamese farms are small. The average agricultural household has just 0.49 hectares of agricultural land (Table 3), and less than 12 percent of rural households have more than 1.0 hectare. The number of rural households with no agricultural land is small, as a result of the relatively equitable process of decollectivization. According to the 1994 Agricultural Census, less than 2 percent of the agricultural households had no land (Table 4).

The problem of landlessness is growing, however, particularly in the Mekong Delta. The 1993 Land Law allows households to sell, lease, mortgage, and inherit land, leading some households to sell or lose their land when unable to repay loans. Official statistics indicate that the proportion of landless households in the Mekong

Table 3—Average farm size and cultivated rice area by region

Region	Agricultural Census (1994) Farm size	VLSS (1992–93) Cultivated rice area	
	(hectare/farm)	(hectare/farm)	(percent of agricultural land)
Northern Uplands	0.43	0.29	58.0
Red River Delta	0.23	0.23	92.9
North Central Coast	0.30	0.27	77.7
South Central Coast	0.41	0.27	69.2
Central Highlands	0.74	0.32	45.2
Southeast	0.92	0.63	85.7
Mekong River Delta	1.10	0.91	92.4
Viet Nam	0.49	0.41	79.8

Sources: Agricultural Census data from GSO 1995b, Vol. 1, 92, 96, 100, 104, 108, 112, 118, 122. Other columns calculated based on data from GSO 1994.

Note: The VLSS figures refer to the average size of *rice-growing* farms.

Table 4—Distribution of households by farm size and by region

Farm size in hectares	Viet Nam	Northern Uplands	Red River Delta	North Central Coast	South Central Coast	Central High-lands	South-east	Mekong Delta
					(percent)			
No land	1.2	0.9	0.8	2.3	1.4	0.8	1.7	0.7
Less than 0.2	27.0	25.5	45.5	30.7	28.0	10.2	9.5	6.2
0.2 to 0.5	44.0	49.1	50.4	54.7	46.2	32.3	27.5	25.7
0.5 to 1.0	16.2	17.2	3.2	11.1	17.6	32.5	29.7	30.7
1 to 3	10.5	6.9	0.1	1.1	6.4	22.9	27.9	32.5
More than 3	1.2	0.5	0.0	0.0	0.4	1.5	2.7	4.4
Total	100.0	100.0	100.0	100.0	100.0	100.0	100.0	100.0

Source: GSO 1995b, Table 2.107.

Note: Numbers may not add to 100 due to rounding.

Table 5—Estimates of labor use in rice production

Region	Pingali et al. 1998	Dung 1994	Dac 1996	IFPRI 1996
		(days/hectare/season)		
Red River Delta	246	—	238	252
Mekong River Delta	96	88	—	89/92
Viet Nam	—	—	—	116/134

Sources: Pingali et al. 1998; Dung 1994; Dac 1996, 49; IFPRI 1996.
Note: The range given for the IFPRI figures refers to the estimates of labor use in different cropping seasons.

Delta has increased from less than 0.7 percent in 1994 to 5.7 percent in 1998 (Nguyen 1999).

Farms tend to be smaller in the north, particularly in the densely populated Red River Delta where the average farm has just 0.22 hectares. In the south, intensive rice cultivation began more recently, so it is less densely populated and the farms tend to be larger. Rice accounts for a majority of the farm area in every region except the Central Highlands (where it is 45 percent). The proportion of land allocated to rice is more than 90 percent in the two deltas (Table 3).

Labor Use

The labor-intensity of rice production also reflects variation in population densities. In the Red River Delta, rice cultivation takes more than 200 person-days per hectare per season, while in the Mekong Delta the corresponding figure is 85 to 100 person-days (Table 5). For the country as a whole, the average labor input is 116 to 134 person-days per hectare per season. This is roughly in the middle of the range found in Asian countries (IRRI 1991).

Farmers in the Red River Delta use more labor in every phase of paddy production. Land preparation in the Red River Delta is more labor-intensive because the use of rented two-wheeled tractors is less common than in the south, though their use is growing in both regions. Furthermore, most Red River Delta farmers use manure, while very few do so in the Mekong Delta. Similarly, planting in the Red River Delta uses four times as much labor per hectare as in the Mekong Delta, largely because Red River farmers transplant rice seedlings rather than broadcasting seed. And harvesting in the Red River Delta is three times as labor intensive as in the Mekong because threshing is less mechanized (Pingali et al.1998).

Another difference between the two deltas is in the use of hired labor in rice production. In the IFPRI farm survey, hired labor represented just 5 percent of total labor use in the Red River Delta, but 33 to 39 percent in the Mekong River Delta (IFPRI 1996). Dac (1996, 49) in the Red River Delta and Dung (1994, 68) in the Mekong Delta obtained similar findings.

Table 6—Estimates of fertilizer use in rice cultivation in Viet Nam

Region	Urea	NPK	SP	Potash	DAP
			(kilograms/hectare)		
Red River Delta	170–200	30–35	196–274	30	0
Mekong River Delta	131–165	88–91	5–34	6–14	40–100

Source: IFPRI 1996.

Notes: The range refers to averages for different seasons. NPK refers to compound fertillizer with nitrogen, phosphorous, and potassium. SP is superphosphate, and DAP is diammonium phosphate.

Rapid economic growth in Viet Nam has implications for rice cultivation practices. With rising opportunity costs in the Mekong Delta, farmers have increased the use of direct seeding and herbicides, while reducing the application of manure. Some of these practices will be adopted elsewhere as wage rates continue to rise (Pingali et al. 1998).

Fertilizer and Pesticide Use

After falling sharply in the late 1970s, chemical fertilizer use has increased dramatically since 1980. Attempts to collectivize agriculture in the south contributed to a reduction in fertilizer consumption from 420,000 tons of plant nutrients in 1977 to 155,000 tons in 1980, equivalent to about 22 kilograms per hectare of agricultural land. With the adoption of the contract system, fertilizer use climbed to 376,000 tons of nutrients (57 kilograms per hectare) in 1983 and to 544,000 tons (85 kilograms per hectare) by 1990. Since 1990, fertilizer use has increased three-fold, reaching 1.5 million tons of nutrients (200 kilograms per hectare) in 1996 (data from the FAOSTAT database of the FAO and GSO 1996b, 367). This growth is attributed to the liberalization of fertilizer imports,[5] falling urea/paddy price ratios,[6] and increasing cropping intensity of rice production.

Taking into account the fact that 75 to 80 percent of the fertilizer is used on paddy and the area sown with paddy, farmers are applying around 170 to 182 kilograms of plant nutrients per sown hectare of paddy. Although application levels are higher in the deltas, the use of chemical fertilizer is not limited to these areas: according to the VLSS, 92 percent of the rice farmers use chemical fertilizers. Table 6 shows some typical fertilizer applications obtained from the IFPRI farm survey.

Organic fertilizers are used by more than two-thirds of the rice farmers in Viet Nam, but there are wide regional differences. The proportion is more than 80 percent

[5] Fertilizer imports were subject to import quotas from 1992 to 1999, though it is not clear how binding these quotas have been. Domestic production increased in the 1990s until the Asian financial crisis in 1997, when Indonesian urea became more competitive.

[6] According to unpublished data from the Ministry of Trade, the retail urea/paddy price ratio fell from 2.1 in 1991 to 1.1 in 1999.

in the north and the South Central Coast but less than 30 percent in the Central Highlands, Southeast, and the Mekong River Delta. The use of organic fertilizer is falling due to the rising opportunity cost of labor and the falling urea/paddy price ratio.

Insecticides are used by most rice farmers, and more than 80 percent of rice farmers in the two deltas own sprayers (Dung 1994, 34; Dac 1996, 32). Weeds are more often controlled by physical methods rather than herbicides. Integrated pest management is a topic of growing importance in research and extension activities.

Cost of Production

The 1995 IFPRI survey of rice farmers collected information on the costs of production, shown in Tables 7 and 8. The cash costs of production represent 34 to 42 percent of the gross revenue from rice production, depending on the season and region. The remainder (58 to 66 percent) is the returns to family labor and family-owned land. Among the purchased inputs, fertilizer is the most important, accounting for 29 to 33 percent of cash costs, followed by seeds, machinery, and land taxes.

Table 8 reveals some regional differences in the composition of production costs. The share of cash expenses allocated to hired labor and machinery expenses is almost twice as high in the Mekong Delta as in the Red River Delta, reflecting differences in cultivation methods discussed above. But rice farmers in the Red River Delta allocate a larger share of cash expenses to animal traction, cooperative fees, and irrigation.

Sources of Rice Production Growth

This section examines the patterns of growth in rice production by decomposing it along several dimensions. First, the contributions of yield, area, and cropping intensity to overall growth are considered. Next, the regional decomposition of rice production growth is examined.

Yield, Area, and Crop Intensity

The growth in production can be decomposed into the growth from each of these three factors plus an interaction term.

$$\frac{\Delta Q}{Q} = \frac{\Delta A}{A} + \frac{\Delta Y}{Y} + \frac{\Delta I}{I} + \textit{interaction}, \tag{1}$$

where Q is production, A is rice area, Y is yield, and I is cropping intensity. The proportional contribution of each factor is calculated by dividing both sides of the equation by $\Delta Q/Q$.

Table 9 shows the increases in cultivated rice area, yield, rice crop intensity, and

Table 7—Cost of production for rice (winter-spring season)

Cost component	Red River Delta		Mekong River Delta		National sample	
	(dong/ kilogram)	(percent of cash cost)	(dong/ kilogram)	(percent of cash cost)	(dong/ kilogram)	(percent of cash cost)
Fertilizer	206	29	162	31	216	33
Pesticides	57	8	46	9	53	8
Seeds	92	13	67	13	90	14
Machinery	50	7	79	15	79	12
Hired labor	35	5	72	14	53	8
Animal traction	64	9	2	0	20	3
Cooperative fees	28	4	2	0	13	2
Irrigation	78	11	21	4	53	8
Land tax	92	13	41	8	66	10
Other	7	1	21	4	20	3
Total cash costs per kilogram	709	100	516	100	662	100

Sources: IFPRI 1996, 308–309.

Table 8—Cost of production for rice (rainy season)

Cost component	Red River Delta		Mekong River Delta		National sample	
	(dong/ kilogram)	(percent of cash cost)	(dong/ kilogram)	(percent of cash cost)	(dong/ kilogram)	(percent of cash cost)
Fertilizer	202	28	225	29	238	31
Pesticides	57	8	54	7	54	7
Seeds	95	13	93	12	106	14
Machinery	57	8	178	23	109	14
Hired labor	36	5	124	16	47	6
Animal traction	71	10	0	0	39	5
Cooperative fees	28	4	0	0	23	3
Irrigation	71	10	8	1	54	7
Land tax	85	12	62	8	93	12
Other	7	1	31	4	16	2
Total cash costs	711	100	776	100	777	100
Farm gate price	2,070		1,866		2,044	

Source: IFPRI 1996, 313–314.

Table 9—Sources of growth in national rice production, 1985–95

Component	Level		Percent change 1985–95	Percent contribution of each factor
	1985	1995		
Rice area (1,000 hectares)	4,297	4,204	-2.2	-3.8
Cropping intensity (ratio)	1.32	1.61	22.0	38.4
Yield (tons/hectare/crop)	2.78	3.69	32.7	57.2
Interaction	—	—	4.7	8.3
Production (1,000 tons)	15,874	24,964	57.3	100.0

Source: GSO 1996b.
Note: Yield and production figures refer to tons of unmilled rice.

paddy production during the period 1985–95. In spite of the 57 percent increase in paddy production (4.6 percent annually), the area devoted to rice cultivation has actually declined slightly. All of the increase in national rice production is due to higher yields and greater cropping intensity. Yields have grown by almost 33 percent (2.9 percent annually), while cropping intensity has risen by 22 percent (2.0 percent annually). This implies that higher yields are responsible for 57 percent of the production growth, while increased crop intensity accounts for 38 percent. The remainder of the production growth is explained by the small decline in cultivated area and the interaction effects.

Regional Patterns in Growth

The production growth rate can be broken down by region using an equation similar to the one used in the previous section. Table 10 indicates that two-thirds of the national growth over this period can be attributed to the Mekong River Delta. Not only did it represent a large share of national paddy production in 1985 (43 percent), but it grew more rapidly than any other region over the 10-year period (87 percent compared with 35 percent for the other six regions). As a result, the Mekong River Delta now accounts for half of national paddy production.

Improvements in irrigation and drainage in the Mekong River Delta have allowed single rice-cropping systems during the rainy season to be converted to double rice-cropping systems, often during the winter-spring and summer-autumn seasons. For example, the areas allocated to floating rice, deep-water rice, and single-crop rainy season rice have declined dramatically in favor of double or even triple rice-cropping systems (Sub-NIAPP 1995).

In the Red River Delta and the North Central Coast, the pattern is quite different. The sown area of rice declined in these regions, so the entire increase in production in these two regions was the result of rising yield. Yield grew close to 50 percent over the 10 years in each of these regions, the highest growth in yield in the country. There

Table 10—Sources of growth in rice production by region, 1985–95

Region	Contribution to regional growth in rice production: Rice area	Cropping intensity	Yield	Interaction	Contribution of region to national growth
			(percent)		
Northern Uplands	20.3	6.3	67.0	6.4	6.1
Red River Delta	-16.3	15.7	102.8	-2.2	16.8
North Central Coast	-16.7	9.0	112.3	-4.6	7.0
South Central Coast	-87.9	149.5	47.7	-9.3	1.5
Central Highlands	-29.8	74.3	55.5	-0.1	0.9
Southeast	14.0	66.9	14.1	4.7	1.9
Mekong River Delta	-1.3	49.9	36.7	14.7	65.7
Viet Nam	-3.8	38.4	57.2	8.3	100.0

Source: Calculated based on data from GSO 1996b.

is little room for area expansion because of the high population density and little scope for further increasing already high cropping-intensity ratios.

Potential for Future Growth

In the Red River Delta, the potential for area expansion is very limited. Not only is agricultural land around Hanoi and Haiphong being absorbed for urban and industrial development, but an increasing share of the land is being allocated to vegetables and other crops as farmers diversify production to meet the demand from urban consumers (Sub-NIAPP 1995, 39). Thus, in the Red River Delta, any increase in paddy production will probably depend on improving yields rather than area expansion or intensification.

In the Mekong River Delta, the conversion of fallow land into land for paddy production in the provinces of Long An and Kien Giang would increase the sown paddy area by 232,000 hectares (Sub-NIAPP 1995). In addition, cropping intensity on existing rice land could be increased, largely through investment in flood control and drainage on the southern coast, where dry-season salinity is a problem. The combined effect would be to increase sown paddy area by 500,000 hectares, representing 7 percent of national sown area.

The potential for yield increases is more difficult to estimate. Average yields have grown 2.8 percent since 1985, reaching 4 tons per hectare in 1999. Historical rates of yield growth, however, may not be sustainable. Among the developing countries in Asia, rice yields grew just 1.3 percent annually over the same period, suggesting that part of Viet Nam's yield growth represents a one-time response to decollectivization and market liberalization. Viet Nam may be following the pattern of China,

Table 11—Rice yields and yield growth in Viet Nam, China, and Asia

Year	Developing Asia	China	Viet Nam
Rice yield (metric tons of paddy/hectare)			
1965	1.99	2.98	1.90
1970	2.27	3.29	2.06
1975	2.41	3.51	2.17
1980	2.74	4.24	2.12
1985	3.27	5.31	2.78
1990	3.56	5.61	3.17
1995	3.74	6.02	3.67
1996	3.87	6.33	3.98
Annual yield growth (percent)			
1965–1975	1.9%	1.7%	1.3%
1975–1985	3.1%	4.2%	2.5%
1985–1999	1.3%	1.4%	2.8%

Source: FAO Agrostat database (http://apps.fao.org/).
Note: Yields are three-year averages centered on the indicated year. Growth rates are based on these three-year averages.

Table 12—Rice yields in selected countries, 1996

Country	Yield
	(kilograms/hectare)
Australia	6.79
Bangladesh	2.79
Cambodia	1.74
China	6.07
Taiwan	5.68
India	2.81
Indonesia	4.51
Japan	6.19
Korea, South	6.10
Laos	2.50
Malaysia	3.13
Myanmar	3.22
Pakistan	2.45
Philippines	2.86
Sri Lanka	2.80
Thailand	2.36
Viet Nam	3.60
United States	6.86

Source: FAOSTAT database of the FAO.

which began liberalization earlier. In China, annual yield growth was more than 4 percent during 1975–85, but has since slowed to 1.4 percent (see Table 11).

Pingali et al. (1998) argue that further increases in Vietnamese yields may be difficult to achieve. For example, fertilizer use expanded rapidly over the 1980s in response to market liberalization, but application rates in the two main deltas are now similar to those in other irrigated regions of Asia. Furthermore, the high yields depend on labor-intensive cultivation methods that farmers may not be willing to continue as wage rates rise. Although the industrialized and newly industrialized countries obtain yields of 5.7 to 6.9 tons per hectare, the only developing countries in Asia with higher yields than Viet Nam are China, with 6.1 tons per hectare, and Indonesia, with 4.5 tons per hectare (Table 12). These two countries have much larger areas under irrigation: 93 and 72 percent, respectively, compared to around 56 percent in Viet Nam (Pingali, Hossain, and Gerpacio 1997, 21). But the average yield in China is still 20 percent higher than in the Red River Delta, which is almost entirely irrigated.

To summarize, there is little scope for expanding sown paddy area significantly so expansion in paddy production will increasingly depend on yield improvements. Although yield growth has been relatively strong over the last 14 years, it seems likely that this is part of a one-time response to liberalization and improved incentives. If this is true, yield growth in Viet Nam will probably decline toward the yield growth rate of other developing countries in Asia.

CHAPTER 3

Structure and Performance of Rice Markets

The Vietnamese marketing system handles an impressive volume of rice: in 1997 about 16 million tons of milled rice were produced, of which 7 to 8 million tons were marketed, passing through the hands of assemblers, millers, wholesalers, transporters, and retailers. At least 2 million tons were shipped from surplus to deficit regions within Viet Nam, and more than 3 million tons were exported. On the one hand, the size of the marketing system is not surprising given the importance of rice as a source of income for farm households, as a staple food, and as a major export. On the other hand, the complexity and sophistication of the marketing system may be somewhat unexpected given that participation in trading activities was suppressed, with varying degrees of harshness, by the government before the *doi moi* policy was introduced in 1986.

The objectives of this chapter are twofold. First, the structure and operation of the "new" rice marketing system in Viet Nam is described, following the various marketing channels that bring the product from farmer to consumer and identifying some of the characteristics of the main participants in the marketing system. Second, the performance of the rice marketing system is assessed. Several types of marketing margins are examined under the assumption that margins will decline if markets become more competitive and traders become more efficient. Prices are analyzed to study changes in the co-movement of prices across markets within Viet Nam. Finally, evidence is presented showing that the rice export quota has been binding, lowering the domestic price of rice, and that internal restrictions limit the flow of rice from south to north, widening the gap in rice prices between these two regions.

Structure of Rice Markets

This section describes the channels by which rice is marketed in Viet Nam and the characteristics of the main participants in this process. It covers farm-level marketing, the milling sector, wholesale marketing, domestic retail marketing, and rice ex-

Table 13—Proportion of rural households growing and selling rice by region

Region	Proportion of rural households growing rice	Proportion of rice farmers selling rice	Proportion of rural households selling rice
		(percent)	
Northern Uplands	94.1	33.6	31.6
Red River Delta	95.0	60.4	57.3
North Central Coast	88.0	40.8	35.9
South Central Coast	82.4	33.3	27.4
Central Highlands	80.9	14.7	11.9
Southeast	57.4	58.5	33.6
Mekong River Delta	73.9	75.5	55.8
Viet Nam	84.5	50.7	42.8

Source: Calculated based on data from the Viet Nam Living Standards Survey, 1992–93.

ports. Given its importance in overall rice markets, the Mekong River Delta's marketing system is discussed in more detail than the other regions.

Farm-Level Marketing

Data from the 1992–93 VLSS indicate that 84 percent of the rural households in Viet Nam grow rice and 43 percent of rural households sell rice or paddy (see Table 13). Thus, half of the Vietnamese rice farmers sell some of their harvest. The high proportion of surplus rice farmers is a reflection of the relatively equitable distribution of land and the fact that Viet Nam is a rice exporter. Furthermore, the proportion of surplus rice farmers is probably even higher than these figures suggest because exports have risen from 2.5 million tons when the survey was carried out to 4.5 million tons in 1999.

The proportion of surplus rice farmers is highest in the Mekong Delta, where three-quarters of the rice farmers sell part of their output. The proportion is more than 50 percent in the Red River Delta and the Southeast, but less than 40 percent in the other regions.

Interestingly, high-income rice farmers are only slightly more likely to generate a marketable surplus than low-income rice farmers (Table 14). Because poor rural households are more likely to grow rice than rich households, the proportion of all rural households that sell rice is actually *higher* among the poor than the rich. This has implications for the impact of rice policy on the poor, as discussed in Chapter 5.

The proportion of rice production that is marketed varies widely across regions, as shown by the results from the VLSS and the IFPRI survey in Table 15. More than two-thirds of the paddy harvested in the Mekong Delta is sold. The Southeast is also highly commercialized. The two surveys show sharply different estimates of the

Table 14—Proportion of rural households growing and selling rice by expenditure category

Expenditure category by quintile	Proportion of rural households growing rice	Proportion of rice farmers selling rice	Proportion of rural households selling rice
		(percent)	
Poorest	91.2	50.1	45.7
2	87.3	46.1	40.2
3	85.6	51.0	43.7
4	82.8	53.4	44.2
Richest	69.5	56.2	39.1
Viet Nam	84.5	50.7	42.8

Source: Calculated from the Viet Nam Living Standards Survey, 1992–93.
Note: Expenditure refers to per capita consumption expenditure (including the value of home-produced food).

Table 15—Rice production per agricultural household, 1995

Region	Paddy production (1)	Agricultural households (2)	Rice production/ agricultural household (3)	Marketed surplus of rice farmers: VLSS 1992/93 (4)	Marketed surplus of rice farmers: IFPRI 1995/96 (5)
	(thousand metric tons)	(thousand of households)	(kilograms)	(rice sales as percent of production)	
Northern Uplands	2,254	1,956	640	19.3	12.0
Red River Delta	4,623	2,647	971	30.3	62.0
North Central Coast	2,141	1,583	752	29.1	33.0
South Central Coast	1,749	1,033	941	24.2	37.0
Central Highlands	429	436	547	10.5	45.0
Southeast	935	591	879	52.5	55.0
Mekong River Delta	12,832	2,297	3,105	65.6	72.0
Viet Nam	24,963	10,543	1,316	43.2	64.0

Sources: Columns (1) and (2) from GSO 1996b, 24, 66. Column (3) calculated assuming 0.65 conversion factor from paddy to rice and 0.855 conversion from rice production to rice available for human consumption. Column (4) calculated from 1992–93 Viet Nam Living Standards Survey (VLSS) data. Column (5) calculated from IFPRI survey of rice farmers (see IFPRI 1996, 59).
Notes: VLSS data probably understate 1995 market surplus ratios because paddy output grew 14 percent between 1992–93 when the survey was carried out and 1995. The IFPRI data probably overstate current market surplus ratios because the sample was focused on specialized rice farmers who tend to be larger than average.

Table 16—Characteristics of traders

Traders	Years of experience	Percentage of time devoted to rice trade	Age	Percentage who are female
Assembler	7.69	92	35	53
Wholesaler	7.58	78	38	71
Retailer	7.55	89	39	80

Source: IFPRI 1996.

marketed surplus for the Red River Delta: 30 percent versus 62 percent. This may be the result of expansion in the market surplus between the two surveys, a period during which the new land law was implemented in the Delta, giving farmers stronger incentives to produce for the market. Alternatively, it may reflect the fact that the IFPRI survey focused on specialized rice farmers who tend to be somewhat larger than average. Both surveys agree, however, that the other regions are much less commercialized, particularly the mountainous areas in the Northern Uplands and the Central Highlands. In these areas, rice production is mostly for home consumption.

Who buys the paddy from farmers? According to the 1995 IFPRI survey of rice farmers, private assemblers account for more than 95 percent of paddy purchases from farmers in every region of the country. This finding contradicts the conventional wisdom in Viet Nam that the SOEs are active at the farm level. Assemblers tend to be relatively young, and slightly more than half are women (Table 16). They almost always operate in a relatively small area, buying from farmers within a distance of 10 kilometers. This allows assemblers to acquire and use a knowledge of the cropping patterns and marketing history of local farmers. The scale of operation, however, is quite small (see Table 17). In the northern and central regions, assemblers use bicycles and "cyclos" (three-wheeled vehicles, either motorized or pedal-operated) to collect the paddy and handle 30 to 100 tons per year. In the south, they use carts and boats, allowing them to move 200 to 1,000 tons per year (IFPRI 1996, 104–125).

In the Mekong Delta, assemblers generally sell paddy to medium- and large-scale millers. In contrast, assemblers in other regions tend to have the paddy milled and sell processed rice to wholesalers. As shown in Figure 2, marketing channels are numerous because assemblers also sell to wholesalers, retailers, and SOEs.

Milling Sector

The rice milling sector is composed of private and state-owned rice mills with a wide range of capacities, as shown in Table 18. Small mills (those having a capacity of less than 1 ton per day) are the most numerous and widespread in Viet Nam. They are almost always privately owned and are operated by just one or two workers. Fre-

Table 17—Size of operation of marketing agents

	Rice sales	Assets
	(metric tons/month)	(US$1,000)
Viet Nam		
Traders	33	3
Millers	171	31
State-owned enterprises	4,017	1,594
Mekong River Delta		
Polishers	800	218
State-owned enterprises	5,054	1,395

Source: IFPRI 1996.

Table 18—Characteristics of millers

Type of miller	Starting year of operation	Tenure of current management	Milling capacity	Polishing capacity	Storage capacity	Number of permanent workers
				(metric tons)		
Small	1991	1991	0.7	0.0	7.6	1.6
Medium	1987	1988	5.9	0.0	123.9	3.5
Large	1985	1988	24.1	0.0	476.5	7.2
Miller/polisher	1986	1987	34.2	38.0	5,650.0	36.0
Polisher	1991	1992	0.0	7.5	2,055.6	23.6

Source: IFPRI 1996.

quently, these mills process paddy on a contract basis for farmers to meet their own consumption needs. Medium-sized mills, processing 1 to 10 tons per day, generally employ 3 to 5 workers. Large mills, defined as those that can process more than 10 tons per day, are generally operated by 5 to 10 workers. These mills are fewer in number and are concentrated in the Mekong River Delta and the Southeast. Rice destined for export is often polished, either by millers or specialized polishers. These mills are large and are found almost exclusively in the south.

In the Mekong Delta, the most common pattern is for medium and large millers to buy paddy from assemblers, process it, and sell rice to wholesalers and SOEs. In the center and north, paddy is more often processed by small and medium-sized mills on a contract basis, either by farmers for their own use or by assemblers for sale to wholesalers (Figure 2).

Figure 2—Rice marketing channels in the Mekong River Delta

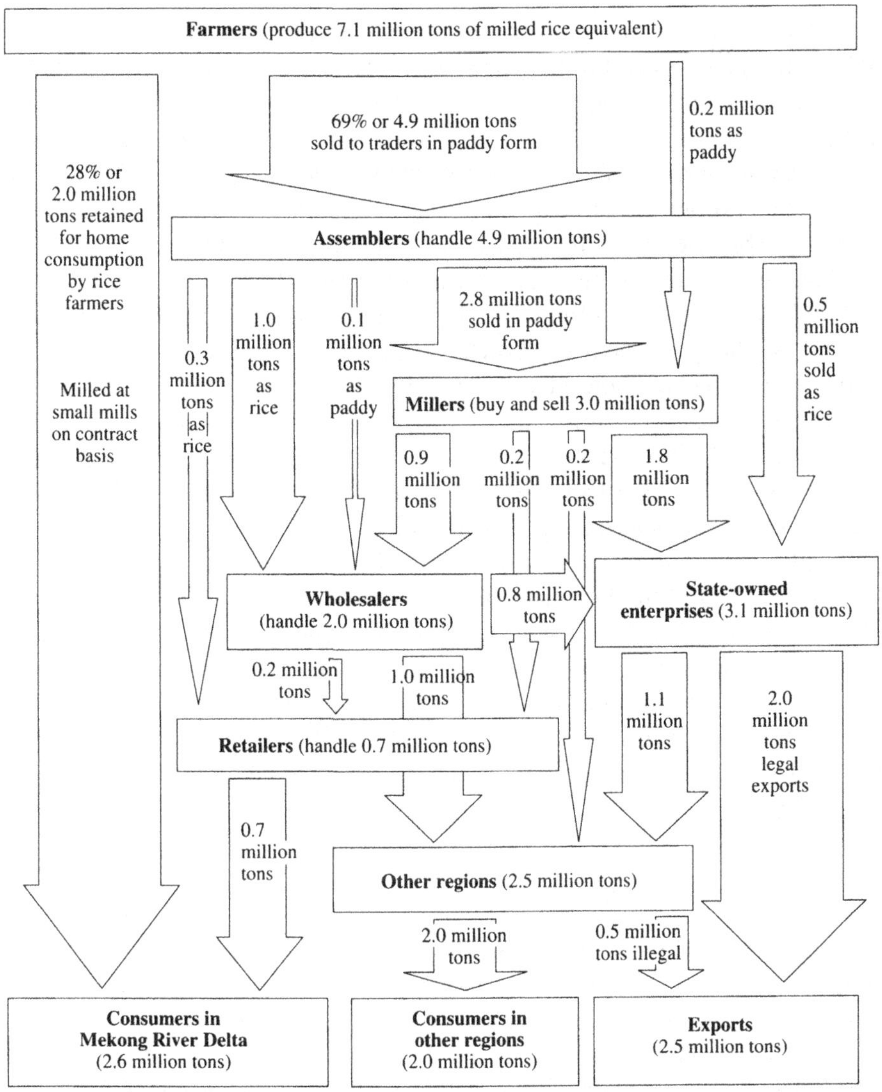

Sources: Production data from GSO (1996) for 1995 crop year. Proportions sold to each marketing agent based on data from 1995-96 IFPRI survey.

Notes: All figures in milled rice equivalent. Thickness of arrows is proportional to volume. Flow of 0.2 million tons from assemblers to other regions is excluded. All tons are metric tons.

Wholesale Marketing

Wholesalers are the main intermediaries between other categories of traders (assemblers and retailers) and millers and SOEs. They tend to be more specialized in rice trade than assemblers and retailers, and they operate on a much larger scale. According to the IFPRI survey, wholesalers in the north and center handle 400 to 700 tons per year and use rented trucks to move their goods. Those in the Mekong River Delta move an average of 1,000 tons per year, using their own boats. Wholesalers in the urbanized Southeast are the largest, handling close to 3,000 tons per year on average. In addition, their storage capacity and rice stocks are much larger than those of assemblers and retailers (Table 19). In the north, wholesalers are predominantly men, while in the south the majority are women.

In the IFPRI survey, wholesalers frequently reported buying rice from and selling rice to other wholesalers. Since the average distance of wholesaler transactions is larger than that of other market participants, this presumably involves sales from a rural wholesaler to an urban one or between wholesalers located in different provinces. Wholesalers also supply retail traders.

SOEs play an important role in wholesale trade. They include regional food companies (VINAFOOD I in the north and VINAFOOD II in the south) and provincial food companies. The SOEs operate on a much larger scale than private traders, in terms of volume of trade, size of assets, and storage facilities (Tables 17 and 19). They tend to dominate long-distance internal trade (from south to north), and they have a legal monopoly on rice exports.[7] As a result, the SOEs are major buyers in the Mekong River Delta and important suppliers of rice to wholesalers in the food-deficit regions (Figure 2).

Domestic Retail Marketing

Rice retailers generally buy rice from wholesalers and transport it to their establishment using bicycles or cyclos. About 80 percent of the rice retailers are women, the proportion being highest in the Mekong Delta (Table 16). In rural areas, they work from a stall in the market place, while in urban areas they may have their own shops. Retailers usually handle 40 to 80 tons per year, although the average is higher in the urbanized Southeast. Their storage capacity is minimal (Table 19).

Export Marketing

Although SOEs have a legal monopoly on rice exports, in order to enforce the rice export quotas, they are required to obtain an export permit that specifies the quantity they can export. Between 10 and 40 SOEs have been issued export permits in recent

---

[7] In 1998, the government established criteria for private traders to be eligible to export rice (Decision 12/TTg of January 1998). In 1999, several private companies received quotas, though for only 4 percent of the total rice exports.

Table 19—Rice storage patterns by type of market participant

Market participant	Capacity	Rice stock	Holding period
	(metric tons)		(days)
Retailer	5.6	1.7	5.8
Wholesaler	117.3	22.3	5.9
Assembler	6.1	0.2	1.3
Small miller	17.9	1.9	2.3
Polisher	1,930.9	480.3	15.6
State-owned enterprises	21,734.3	2,978.5	23.2

Source: IFPRI 1996.

Table 20—Vietnamese rice exports and share of world exports

Year	World rice exports	Vietnamese rice exports	Vietnamese share in world exports
	(million metric tons)		(percent)
1989	15.2	1.4	9.3
1990	12.5	1.6	13.0
1991	13.2	1.0	7.9
1992	16.1	1.9	12.1
1993	16.8	1.7	10.2
1994	18.0	2.0	11.0
1995	22.5	2.0[a]	8.8
1996	20.4	3.0	17.2
1997	20.9	3.6	17.1
1998	28.6	3.8	13.3

Source: FAOSTAT database of the FAO.

[a] Official statistics for 1995 give 2.0 million metric tons, but it is widely believed that 0.5 million metric tons were exported "informally" to China that year.

years. The volume of rice exported was around 2 million tons from 1989 to 1995, although it is thought that there were significant "informal" exports to China in 1995 (Table 20). The export quota and the system of administrative allocation of the permits have been the subject of considerable debate in Viet Nam, as will be discussed later in this chapter and in Chapter 6.

Most export-oriented SOEs buy rice rather than paddy, though they may further mill it or polish it before exporting. In some cases, the SOE merely acts as the "official" exporter for a deal arranged between a private miller and a foreign buyer.

Performance of the Rice Marketing System

This section examines the performance of rice markets along several dimensions. First, the trends in the level and variability of rice prices in Viet Nam are reviewed. Second, changes in rice marketing margins and in the degree of spatial integration of rice markets are assessed. Third, the marketing costs and profitability of rice marketing activities are examined. Finally, evidence is presented of policy restrictions on rice trade by combining information on price differences and marketing costs. The analysis is mostly based on time-series data on prices from the General Statistical Office and primary data obtained from the IFPRI surveys in 1995–96.

Trends in Rice Prices

The trends in paddy and rice prices during the period 1989–96 are shown in Table 21. While the average annual increase in rice prices in the first two years of this period (1989–91) was 58 percent, the annual increase fell to under 10 percent for the remaining period (1991–96), reflecting the fall in inflation since 1991. The incentives for paddy production and consumption depend, however, not on nominal prices, but on the prices of paddy and rice relative to other goods. Since 1989 both paddy and rice prices have risen more slowly than the index of retail prices. The real price of paddy has fallen 4.3 percent per year, while the real price of rice has declined 3.2 percent (Table 21). Monthly data presented in Figure 3 show that the decline occurred between mid-1990 and mid-1992. This trend benefits consumers, but the implications for farm income are more difficult to assess. The change in farm income depends on the path of prices, production, and cost of production. As mentioned, real paddy prices have declined by 3.2 percent per year, but production has increased at an annual rate of 5.6 percent over the same period. Reliable trends on cost of production are not available, but yields have grown more than 2.5 percent per year over this period. This suggests that higher productivity has partly compensated for the decline in real prices. Although the net effect on farmers is not clear, the gains to farmers have been lower than they would have been under a more open trade system (as will be shown in Chapter 6). The rice export quota has imposed an implicit tax on Vietnamese rice farmers that has prevented domestic rice prices from reaching parity with export prices.

Variability in Rice Prices

Inflation and related macroeconomic instability in the late 1980s caused rice prices to be quite volatile. As macroeconomic stability returned in the early 1990s, the volatility of rice prices decreased (Figure 4). The coefficient of variation of monthly rice prices was 0.05 during 1991–95, less than one-fifth of the value during 1986–90.

Another source of variability in rice prices is seasonality. At the aggregate level, seasonality is not very pronounced. Over the period 1991–96 the range between seasonal peak and trough was about 10 percent (Figure 5). The seasonal variation is

Table 21—Trends in paddy and rice prices

Year	Farm gate paddy price	Retail rice price	Index retail price	Deflated paddy price	Deflated rice price
	(dong/kilogram)		(1989 = 1.0)	(1989 dong/kilogram)	
1989	497	771	1.0	497	771
1990	833	1,279	1.4	605	930
1991	1,404	1,924	2.5	559	765
1992	1,472	2,020	3.5	426	585
1993	1,445	2,062	3.7	389	556
1994	1,523	2,179	4.1	375	536
1995	1,939	2,761	4.7	411	585
1996	1,822	3,057	5.0	366	614
Annual growth rate, 1989–1996 (percent)	20.4	21.8	25.8	-4.3	-3.2

Source: Monthly District Prices, General Statistical Office; Index Retail Price, Government Price Committee.
Note: Growth rates are based on semi-logarithmic trends.

Figure 3—Real prices of paddy and rice

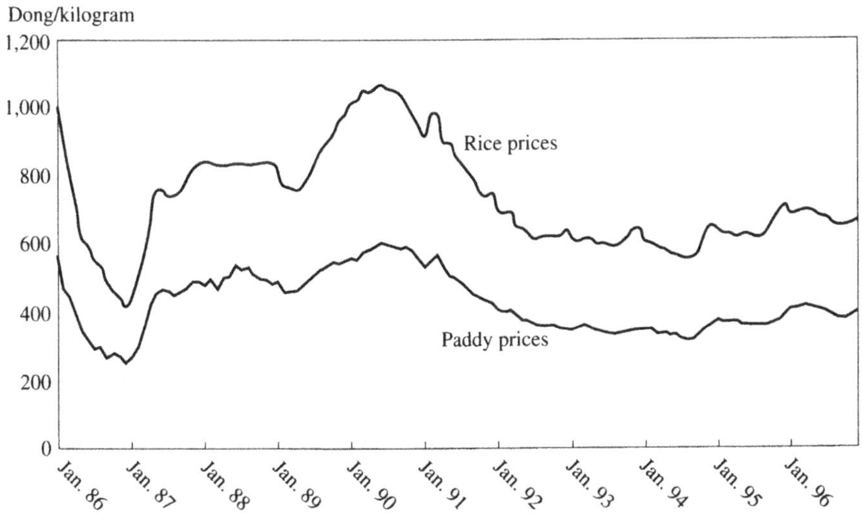

Source: Unpublished data from the General Statistical Office.

Figure 4—Coefficient of variation of monthly paddy prices

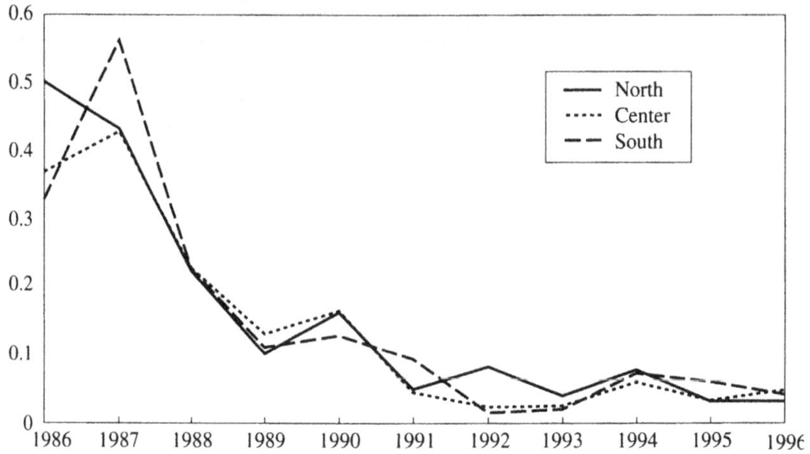

Source: Calculated from unpublished price data from the General Statistical Office.

Figure 5—Seasonal variation in paddy prices

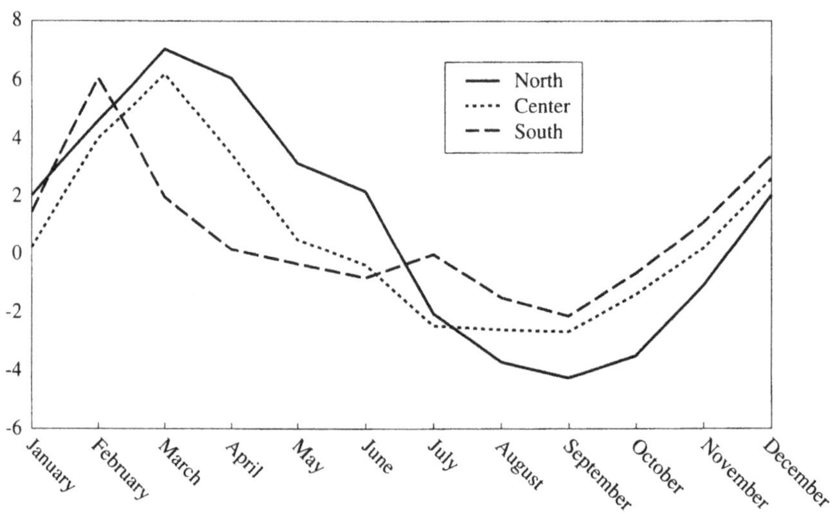

Source: Calculated from unpublished data from the General Statistical Office.

Table 22—Trends in different types of margins

Type of margin	Average margin	Trend
	(percent)	
Margin between rice prices in the north and the south	30	none
Margin between wholesale rice and paddy price in		
North	73	none
South	75	none
Margin between wholesale paddy price and farm price in		
North	5	none
South	4	none
Margin between retail rice price and wholesale price in		
North	8	negligible
South	9	negligible

Source: Based on unpublished data from the General Statistical Office.

Notes: The average margin is the difference between the two relevant prices as a percentage of the lower price. The trend is computed by testing the hypothesis H_1: $ß < 0$ in the regression equation abs($P^1_t - P^2_t$) = $a + ß\,t + \varepsilon_t$ where P^1_t, P^2_t are the relevant prices at time t.

somewhat lower in the south (8 percent) than in the north (12 percent). The aggregate picture, however, hides considerable variation at the district level, where it is possible to have seasonal variation of 30 percent.

Seasonality of price is a reflection of seasonality of production, with prices showing a tendency to decline after harvest and to increase before harvest. The smaller seasonal price variation in the south presumably occurs because the harvest is less seasonally concentrated (see Table 2), and the export market prevents Mekong harvest prices from falling below a certain level.

Trends in Marketing

Marketing margins reflect both the cost of marketing and the profits of marketing agents. Competitive pressure as a result of liberalization of agricultural markets since 1986 can be expected to reduce profits and perhaps costs, resulting in lower marketing margins. This section examines the trends in paddy-rice wholesale price margins, farmer-retail margins, and north-south margins during 1986–95. The analysis shows that very little, if anything, has happened to reduce the price differentials between stages of processing and marketing or across regions.

The paddy-rice price margin reflects the costs and profits in the rice milling sector. Rice prices are 73 to 75 percent above paddy prices in the same location. Regression analysis of the absolute price difference as a function of time show no statistically significant trend over the period 1986–95 (Table 22).

Table 23—Wholesale prices of rice in different regions

Year	Average wholesale price			Margin relative to price in south	
	North	Center	South	North	Center
	(dong/kilogram)			(percent)	
1986	20	20	21	-4.8	-4.8
1987	142	125	124	14.5	0.8
1988	528	441	373	41.6	18.2
1989	779	703	640	21.7	9.8
1990	1,335	1,231	929	43.7	32.5
1991	2,081	1,745	1,499	38.8	16.4
1992	2,111	1,789	1,721	22.7	4.0
1993	2,100	1,840	1,833	14.6	0.4
1994	2,174	2,034	1,818	19.6	11.9
1995	2,917	2,503	2,208	32.1	13.4
1996	3,462	2,919	2,287	51.4	27.6

Source: Based on unpublished data from the General Statistical Office.

The farm-wholesale and wholesale-retail rice price margins reflect changes in the costs and profits of rice trading. Wholesale rice prices are 4 to 5 percent above farm gate rice prices and retail prices are 8 to 9 percent above wholesale prices. Regression analysis again shows no statistically significant trend in the absolute price differences.

Finally, the north-south wholesale rice price margin reflects the costs and profits of transportation and marketing from south to north, given that the deficit regions in the north are supplied annually with part of the surplus from the Mekong Delta. Prices in the north are, on average, 30 percent higher than in the south, but again there is no trend in the price difference over time. Table 23 shows a substantial annual variation in this margin. In addition, as discussed later in this chapter, the north-south margin is larger than would be expected based on marketing and transportation costs. This appears to be the result of policies that restrict interregional trade.

Analysis of Market Integration

The idea behind the analysis of market integration is to study the degree of co-movement of prices in spatially separated markets. A high degree of market integration suggests that the markets are "connected," but this connection is neither necessary nor sufficient for market efficiency. As is well known, efficient markets will be unintegrated if the price difference (in the absence of trade) is less than the cost of transportation between the markets or if flows move in different directions at different

Table 24—Changes in market integration over time

Type of analysis	Measures of market integration	1986–90	1991–95
Correlation analysis	Average correlation of price levels across market pairs	0.98	0.77
	Average correlation of price changes across market pairs	0.40	0.43
Co-integration analysis	Percentage of cointegrated market pairs	29%	39%
	Percentage of segmented market pairs	34%	20%
Dynamic multiplier analysis	Magnitude of price adjustment	0.44	0.54
	Speed of price adjustment	5.15 months	5.34 months

Source: Calculated from unpublished data from General Statistical Office on monthly wholesale rice prices for 1986–95 for 21 districts.

times. Alternatively, markets may be highly integrated even if market power or policy restrictions make the price differences exceed transportation costs (Harriss 1979; Baulch 1997). Nonetheless, the measures of price integration show the degree of connectedness of markets, and changes in the degree of integration should reflect changes in efficiency or transportation costs or both.

There are various approaches to measuring market integration: correlation analysis, cointegration analysis, and dynamic multiplier analysis (see Appendix 1, which discusses the various methods). These methods are applied to monthly data on wholesale rice prices in 21 markets covering the period 1986–95. Each analysis is carried out separately for two periods, 1986–90 and 1991–95, to identify changes in the degree of market integration.

The simplest approach to market integration is to calculate the correlation coefficient for prices in each pair of markets. As shown in Table 24, the average correlation among the 410 market pairs is very high: 0.98 during 1986–90 and 0.77 during 1991–95. This is not surprising, given that all prices were affected by inflation and seasonal patterns. The closer correlation of prices in 1986–90 is due to the higher rate of inflation in that period.

The effect of inflation and seasonal patterns can be removed by analyzing the correlation of price *differences* from one month to the next. This not only reduces the level of correlation substantially, but the degree of correlation increases slightly from the first period to the second (Table 24) Thus, correlation analysis suggests that wholesale rice prices move in line with general inflation, and that price changes are only weakly related among spatially separated markets.

While correlation analysis measures the co-movement of prices in the same month, cointegration analysis takes into account the possible lagged effect of prices in one market on prices in the other and controls for autocorrelation of prices. The

Table 25—Comparative dynamic indicators of market integration

Indicator	Egypt wheat	Bangladesh rice	Malawi maize	Pakistan wheat	Viet Nam rice
Long-term multiplier	0.35	0.73	0.49	0.47	0.54
Speed of adjustment	3.53	2.6	5.7	3.39	5.15

Source: Computations based on General Statistical Office data and Goletti 1994.

analysis of cointegration coefficients shows that the proportion of segmented[8] market links fell from 34 percent in 1986–90 to 20 percent in 1991–95, while the proportion of cointegrated links rose from 29 to 39 percent between the two periods (Table 24). This is an indication that the market reforms have improved long-term relations among various markets.

The analysis of dynamic multipliers provides insight into the extent of integration, by measuring the strength and the speed of the price adjustment process. The analysis shows that the magnitude of the long-term multipliers rose from 0.44 in 1986–90 to 0.54 in 1991–95. The adjustment period is somewhat longer in the second period (5.34 months) than in the first (5.15 months), though the difference is small (see Table 24). International comparison shows that the very low degree of spatial market integration of Viet Nam is similar to that of Malawi, with its poor rural infrastructure, and to that of Pakistan and Egypt, countries that impose restrictions on internal trade (Table 25).

In summary, markets are still poorly integrated in Viet Nam even though there has been a slight improvement over the past decade. Notwithstanding active private sector involvement in rice marketing, the local nature of domestic trade makes it difficult to use arbitrage to minimize the price differentials across spatially separated markets.

Marketing Costs and Profitability

Price incentives, together with marketing costs, affect the profits of marketing agents and thus their procurement and selling decisions. One of the objectives of analyzing costs is to understand the relative efficiency of various marketing agents. The first conclusion emerging from this analysis is that private sector costs are considerably lower than those of SOEs. Unit costs of SOEs in the Mekong River Delta and the Red River Delta range from 4 to 16 times the corresponding costs in the private sector (Table 26). The inefficiency of SOEs is not surprising given the rigidities of em-

[8] Two markets are segmented if there is no long-term relation with each other. In other words two segmented markets are not cointegrated (also see Appendix 1).

Table 26—Unit operating costs

Region	Wholesaler	Medium miller	Large miller and polisher	State-owned enterprise
		(US$/metric ton)		
Red River Delta	7.85	3.26	8.24	55.26
Mekong River Delta	11.67	6.29	7.29	42.99
Viet Nam	9.38	5.88	10.63	40.71

Source: IFPRI 1996.

Table 27—Composition of retail price

Item	Red River Delta		Mekong River Delta	
	(US$/ metric ton)	(percent of retail price)	(US$/ metric ton)	(percent of retail price)
Farmers				
Unit cost	206	65	120	40
Unit profit	57	18	93	31
Farm gate price	263	83	213	71
Market agents				
Unit cost	19	6	33	11
Unit profit	34	11	55	18
Margin	53	17	88	29
Retail price	316	100	301	100

Source: IFPRI 1996.
Note: "Profit" in this table refers to returns to labor and fixed factors such as land.

ployment in the state sector, the lower incentives of salaried managers, and the use of large-scale but often inappropriate equipment. Even so, the extent of the difference is surprising.

A second conclusion emerging from this analysis is that the margins of marketing agents in the Red River Delta are lower than those in the Mekong River Delta (Table 27). This is true whether the margin is defined in absolute terms (US$53 versus US$88 per ton) or as a percentage of the retail price (17 percent versus 29 percent). The higher marketing costs in the Mekong River Delta are a reflection of a more complex marketing system than in the north, characterized by higher transportation, labor, and depreciation costs.

This does not imply, however, that the returns to farmers are lower in the Mekong than in other regions, nor that the prices paid by consumers are higher. The returns to labor in the Mekong are higher than in other regions because yields are high and farms are large by Vietnamese standards. Furthermore, because of the productivity of rice production in the Mekong, consumers pay lower prices for rice in spite of the somewhat higher marketing margin.

Restrictions on Internal Rice Trade

As a result of the deficit position in the north and the surplus in the south, prices in the north are generally higher than prices in the south. In 1995, the wholesale rice prices in the north and in the south were, on average, 2,917 dong[9] per kilogram and D2,208 per kilogram, respectively, implying a price differential of D709 per kilogram or 32 percent of the southern price. As shown in Table 23, this is not an unusual situation: average yearly rice prices in the north were 15 to 39 percent higher than corresponding prices in the south during the period 1987–96.

The IFPRI survey of traders collected data on the costs of transportation and marketing between markets. According to these results, the cost of shipping rice from the south to the north should be slightly less than D300 per kilogram. In other words, only 42 percent of the north-south price difference can be explained by marketing and transportation costs. This suggests that movement restrictions prevent spatial arbitrage from bringing the price differences down to the cost of transportation and marketing.

This hypothesis is supported by the results of the IFPRI trader survey in which traders report restrictions on internal rice trade, particularly on long-distance trade. Almost 60 percent of SOEs report restrictions on internal trade, followed by about 20 percent of miller-polishers, polishers, wholesalers, and assemblers; and less than 10 percent of retailers and millers (Table 28). These patterns reflect the larger volumes and the longer distances over which SOEs, large private traders, miller-polishers, and polishers operate. Retailers and millers generally do not trade over long distances so they do not experience restrictions on the movement of rice.

In part, these restrictions take the form of bureaucratic rigidities. As of late 1996, the procedures to buy and transport rice from the south to the north resemble those for trade with another country. At that time, SOEs in the north wishing to buy rice from the south had to (1) apply for a license from the Ministry of Agriculture and Rural Development, (2) register with the Market Control Department, (3) buy rice at the place determined by VINAFOOD II, (4) register with local market control sections in the south, (5) register at the ports of departure and arrival, and (6) register with local market control sections in the north. These complex procedures add to costs and limit the effective stabilization of food markets in the country. The effect of liberalizing internal rice trade on prices and income are analyzed in Chapter 5, using a simulation model of Vietnamese rice markets.

---

[9] The exchange rate between the dong (VND), the currency of Viet Nam, and the U.S. dollar was 11,032 VND per U.S. dollar.

Table 28—Traders, state-owned enterprises, and millers' reported restrictions on the movement of goods

Agent	Percentage of marketing agents reporting restrictions	Most commonly reported restriction	Second most commonly reported restriction
Retailers	1	Police	Interprovince
Wholesalers	23	Interprovince	Police
Assemblers	17	Interdistrict	Interprovince
State-owned enterprises	57	Interprovince	Police
Small millers	1	Interprovince	Interdistrict
Medium millers	5	Interprovince	Interdistrict
Large millers	5	Interprovince	Interdistrict
Polishers	20	Police	Interprovince
Polishers and millers	24	Interprovince	Interdistrict

Source: IFPRI 1996.

Restrictions on Rice Exports

The policy restrictions on rice exports are more explicit. Since 1989 when Viet Nam began exporting rice, the government has restricted the volume of rice exports through the use of export licenses, even as international trade in other commodities has been liberalized. Government officials argue that the quotas are necessary to ensure adequate domestic supplies and reduce price volatility. In order to control rice exports, only a limited number of SOEs are allocated rice export quotas (the number varies between 15 and 40).

An important question is whether the export quota has been binding. In other words, are rice exports less than what they would be in the absence of the quota? The intense political lobbying among SOEs and private companies to receive export quota allocations would suggest that the quota is binding, but it would be useful to quantify its effect.

According to trade theory, a binding export (import) quota will result in domestic prices below (above) the relevant border price and have similar effects as an export (import) tax. In 1995, the average wholesale price of rice in the Mekong River Delta was D2,231 per kilogram or US$202 per ton, yet the average f.o.b. price of Vietnamese rice exports was US$269 per ton. Thus, the export quota in 1995 was equivalent to an export tax of roughly US$67 per ton or 25 percent of the border price. Table 29 reveals that 1995 was not an unusual year in terms of the divergence between domestic and border prices. This indicates that the rice export quota was binding over the period 1990–95 and equivalent to an export tax of 20 to 25 percent.

Looking toward the future, Viet Nam's rice export policy may be affected by trade agreements over the next 5 to 10 years. Viet Nam's membership in the Association of

Table 29—Margin between domestic and border prices

Year	Domestic price (wholesale price in the Mekong Delta)	Border price (f.o.b. export price)	Margin as percentage of domestic price	Margin as percentage of border price
	(US$/metric ton)		(percent)	
1990	135	170	26.3	20.8
1991	164	226	38.2	27.6
1992	155	207	33.1	24.9
1993	159	203	28.1	21.9
1994	162	218	34.2	25.5
1995	202	269	33.2	24.9
Average	163	216	32.0	24.5

Source: Export and domestic prices from the General Statistical Office.

Southeast Asian Nations (ASEAN), and agreement to the ASEAN Free Trade Agreement (AFTA) is not likely to impose restrictions on Vietnamese rice policy because rice is considered too politically sensitive in most ASEAN countries. Although the World Trade Organization, to which Viet Nam has applied for membership, prohibits the use of export quotas, Dao (1999) argues that current rice policy could be retained under Clause 2(a) of Article 11, which allows "temporary prohibition or restriction of exports to prevent or reduce scarcity of grain, food, or other essential products." On the other hand, Anderson (1998) argues that "WTO members are likely to demand that the quantitative restrictions on rice exports be at least converted to an export tax," except in times of shortage. Thus, WTO commitments highlight the importance of understanding the impact of rice export liberalization, a topic examined in Chapter 6.

Conclusions

This brief description of the structure of the rice marketing system in Viet Nam suggests that it has rapidly developed into a complex system without the central management that policymakers once thought necessary. Tens of thousands of traders handle millions of tons of rice every year, channeling it from surplus farmers to urban consumers, rural rice-deficit areas, and exporters. Furthermore, the channels are numerous and differ from one region to another. The role of the SOEs is minimal in the rice marketing system except in the area of long-distance trade, where it dominates, and exports, where it has a legal monopoly.[10]

Regarding the performance of the rice marketing system, macroeconomic stabilization has reduced rice price volatility, but market liberalization does not seem to

[10] As mentioned earlier, private traders have been allocated export quotas starting in 1999, but they account for just 4 percent of rice exports.

have had a noticeable effect on marketing margins between paddy and rice prices, between farmer and retail prices, or between prices in the north and south. Spatial market integration analysis indicates that the degree of market integration has increased somewhat since the late 1980s, but it remains weak.

The performance of the marketing system is affected by two types of restrictions on trade. First, restrictions on internal trade were in effect in 1995, as indicated by the responses of traders in the 1995–96 IFPRI survey and by the large price differential between rice prices in the north and south. Second, the rice export quota is used by the government to ensure adequate domestic supplies. A comparison of domestic and border prices reveals that the quota was binding at least during 1990–95 and that it was equivalent to an export tax of 20 to 25 percent. The implications of these policies and some alternatives are presented in Chapter 6.

CHAPTER 4

Food Demand and Calorie Consumption

Information on food and caloric consumption patterns is useful in the analysis of rice policy for several reasons. First, the impact of rice policy on the welfare of different households depends in part on the importance of rice in their budgets. Second, in order to simulate the impact of policy changes on rice markets, information is needed on the price and income elasticities of demand for rice and other foods. Third, the relationship between income and rice consumption is critical for evaluating the sustainability of Vietnamese rice exports, especially given the constraints on expanding rice production discussed in Chapter 2. Finally, even though rice is the main food staple in Viet Nam, other foods contribute to total calorie consumption. The effect of price changes on total calorie consumption is critical to evaluate the effects of policy on food security, particularly for the poorest.

This chapter first describes the trends in rice consumption over time. Then patterns of rice consumption and purchases across regions and household types are examined; an econometric model of food demand in Viet Nam, of which rice is a part, is estimated; and the effects of price and income changes on total calorie consumption are evaluated.

Trends in Rice Consumption

The only data on Vietnamese rice consumption available for various years is apparent rice consumption per capita, defined as net production minus net exports divided by population.[11] It is assumed that postharvest losses, seed, and feed account for 14.5 percent of production.[12] The limitations of this measure of con-

[11] Production statistics, expressed in terms of paddy, are converted to milled rice equivalents using a conversion factor of 0.65. Trade statistics are already expressed in terms of milled rice.

[12] This is based on an estimate by Le Don Dien (1995). This percentage is roughly consistent with data from the 1998 Viet Nam Living Standards Survey in which 12 percent of the rice harvest was used for seed, fed to animals, or lost (GSO 1999, Table 5.2.6). In addition, the apparent consumption figures derived from this estimate are consistent with survey-based estimates of per capita rice consumption (compare Tables 30 and 31).

sumption are well known, but it should provide a rough indicator of trends in rice consumption.[13]

During the 1960s and early 1970s, the south imported between 100,000 and 500,000 tons of rice per year. After the unification of Viet Nam in 1975, rice imports practically disappeared, causing a sharp reduction in apparent consumption. This was partly related to the military and economic withdrawal of the United States during 1973–75 and partly due to the emphasis placed on self-sufficiency by the socialist government that took control of the south in 1975.

The five-year plan of 1976–81 called for a 40 percent increase in staple food production. Nonetheless, attempts to collectivize agriculture in the south actually resulted in lower output, with production and apparent consumption reaching a low point of less than 110 kilograms per capita in 1978. With the relaxation of attempts to collectivize the south, consumption recovered to about 125 kilograms in 1980–81, but this was still far below the target.

In 1981, Instruction 100 allowed farmers to cultivate individual plots and sell above-quota surpluses on the free market. These partial reforms raised production in the next five years to about 170 kilograms per capita and consumption to around 150 kilograms per capita, bringing consumption back to its wartime level and production above that level.

In 1988 and 1989, Instruction 10, which effectively decollectivized agricultural production, combined with trade liberalization and devaluation, improved the incentives to produce and export rice (Pingali and Xuan 1992). Production per capita rose fairly steadily from 173 kilograms in 1988 to 233 kilograms in 1997. This allowed exports to expand, reaching 45 kilograms per capita in 1997.

In the first two years of rice exports (1989–90), the absolute increase in rice exports was greater than the absolute increase in rice production, resulting in lower apparent consumption. Starting in 1991, however, apparent rice consumption rose from around 146 kilograms to 154 kilograms per capita by 1997 in spite of the growing exports. Overall, the expansion of rice exports since 1988 has not occurred through the reduction of domestic consumption. Rather, increased production has allowed dramatic expansion of exports combined with smaller increases in domestic per capita rice consumption (Table 30).

It is interesting to note that apparent per capita rice consumption is relatively stable over the 1990s. Given that per capita gross domestic product increased at about 6 percent annually over this period, the implication is that the income elasticity of rice demand is close to zero.[14]

---

[13] This measure of apparent consumption does not, however, take into account the level of stocks from one year to the next. Changes in stocks tend to be positive in high-production years and negative in low-production years. Thus, to the extent that changes in stocks are significant, actual consumption will be more stable over time than apparent consumption.

[14] Real rice prices have been relatively stable since 1992 (see Figure 3) and the pace of urbanization is relatively slow in Viet Nam, so these factors are not likely to have had much effect on demand trends over the 1990s.

Table 30—Apparent rice consumption in Viet Nam, 1975–97

Year	Paddy production	Rice production per capita	Net exports of rice	Population	Apparent rice consumption
	(million metric tons)	(kilograms per capita)	(million metric tons)	(millions)	(kilograms per capita)
1975	10.5	144	-0.3	47.6	130
1976	11.8	156	-0.1	49.2	137
1977	10.6	137	-0.2	50.4	121
1978	9.8	124	-0.1	51.4	107
1979	11.4	141	-0.1	52.5	122
1980	11.6	141	-0.2	53.7	124
1981	12.4	147	0.0	54.9	126
1982	14.4	167	-0.2	56.2	146
1983	14.7	167	0.0	57.4	143
1984	15.5	172	-0.2	58.7	151
1985	15.9	172	-0.3	59.9	152
1986	16.0	170	-0.4	61.1	151
1987	15.1	157	-0.2	62.5	138
1988	17.0	173	-0.1	63.7	150
1989	19.0	191	1.4	64.8	142
1990	19.2	189	1.6	66.2	137
1991	19.6	188	1.0	67.8	146
1992	21.6	202	1.9	69.4	145
1993	22.8	209	1.7	71.0	154
1994	23.5	211	2.0	72.5	153
1995	24.9	219	2.0	74.0	160
1996	26.5	228	3.0	75.5	155
1997	27.6	233	3.5	77.0	154

Source: For data until 1995, paddy production and population from Kim 1996, and net export data from the FAOSTAT database of the FAO. For 1996 and 1997 data based on communication from the General Statistical Office. Rice production calculated from paddy production assuming 65 percent conversion. Apparent consumption calculated from paddy production assuming 65 percent conversion and 14.5 percent losses, seedand feed use.

Rice Consumption across Households

Rice consumption was measured at the household level by the Viet Nam Living Standards Survey (VLSS) in 1992–93. The VLSS used a nationally representative sample of 4,800 households scattered across 150 communes in 52 of the 54 provinces. The survey collected information on income, expenditure, housing, health, education, migration, agricultural production, and food consumption, among other topics. The information presented in this section is based on a subsample of 4,513 households from the VLSS.[15]

According to the VLSS, rice is consumed by practically every household in Viet Nam (99.9 percent). The data from the survey indicate that in 1992–93 average rice consumption was 156 kilograms per capita. This figure corresponds fairly closely to the per capita apparent consumption in 1992 and 1993 (Table 30).

Rice is by far the most important food item in Viet Nam. As shown in Table 31, rice contributes 75 percent of the caloric intake of Vietnamese households and represents almost 30 percent of the value of consumption expenditure.[16] By contrast, the three minor staples (maize, cassava, and sweet potatoes) together represent less than 8 percent of the value of consumption expenditure and less than 4 percent of the caloric intake.

Rice consumption does vary, however, across household types, as shown in Table 31. Urban households consume about 127 kilograms of rice per capita, compared with 163 kilograms per capita in rural areas. Households headed by males consume somewhat more rice than households headed by females (157 to 151 kilograms per capita), largely because female-headed households are more common in urban areas.

Regionally, rice consumption ranges from 131 kilograms per capita in the Southeast to close to 170 kilograms per capita in the Red River Delta. Part of these differences can be attributed to the effects of urbanization and income. The Southeast has the highest average income and is the most urbanized of the seven regions.

Rice consumption also varies by income group, as shown in Table 31 and Figure 6. At low levels of income,[17] rice is a normal good (rice consumption rises with income). But beyond a certain level of income, however, rice consumption begins to fall, making rice an inferior good. In this income range, additional income is not spent on rice but rather on higher-value foods such as meat, eggs, and dairy products and on nonfood items (see GSO 1994, 194).

The share of the budget allocated to rice falls from 47 percent in the poorest quintile to just 12 percent in the richest. Similarly, the share of calories coming from rice falls with higher incomes, but even in the richest quintile, rice contributes more than half of the caloric intake.

---

[15] Households for which estimated caloric intake was below 1,000 kilocalories per person or above 3,500 kilocalories per person were excluded from the analysis, based on the idea that these figures reflect problems in the consumption data.

[16] Consumption expenditure is the total value of purchases for consumption, food produced and consumed within the household, goods obtained through barter or gift, and the rental equivalent of consumer durables and housing.

[17] Throughout the analysis of the Viet Nam Living Standards Survey, this study uses per capita consumption expenditure as the main indicator of the well-being of households. It is easier than income to measure accurately and more stable over time. Nonetheless, in the interest of simplicity, the term "income" is used in the text.

Table 31—Rice consumption by household type

Household type	Percentage of all households	Rice consumption	Value of rice consumption	Calories from rice
	(percent)	(kilograms/person/ year)	(percent of total consumption expenditure)	(percent of total caloric intake)
Viet Nam	100.0	155.6	29.6	75.2
Sex of household head				
Male	73.2	157.3	30.6	76.0
Female	26.8	150.9	26.9	72.8
Location				
Urban	20.0	126.9	17.1	62.0
Rural	80.0	162.8	32.7	78.4
Region				
Northern Uplands	16.7	155.5	34.8	74.8
Red River Delta	24.0	169.5	34.8	79.3
North Central Coast	13.3	152.6	33.9	76.9
South Central Coast	11.3	145.5	25.6	73.7
Central Highlands	2.7	161.9	32.6	77.6
Southeast	11.3	131.1	19.0	64.5
Mekong River Delta	20.7	159.7	24.3	75.8
Income quintile				
Poorest	20.0	148.2	46.9	81.6
2nd	20.0	157.2	37.3	81.8
3rd	20.0	164.8	29.8	79.1
4th	20.0	163.3	22.0	73.2
Richest	20.0	144.7	12.0	60.1

Source: Calculated from Viet Nam Living Standards Survey 1992–93 data.

Determinants of Food Demand

In this section, regression analysis is used to examine systematically the determinants of the demand for food among Vietnamese households. The linear approximation of the Almost Ideal Demand System (AIDS) is used with an urban-expenditure interaction term to allow greater flexibility in demand patterns between urban and rural households. Thus, the demand equation takes the following form:

$$s_i = a_i + \sum_{j=1}^{14} \beta_{ij} \ln(p_j) + (\gamma_i + \theta_i Z_0) \ln \frac{x}{P} + \sum_{k=1}^{11} \delta_{ik} Z_k, \tag{2}$$

where s_i is the budget share of food group i, p_j is the price of food j, Z_0 is a dummy variable indicating urban households, x is the value of consumption expenditure per

Figure 6—Rice consumption by expenditure decile

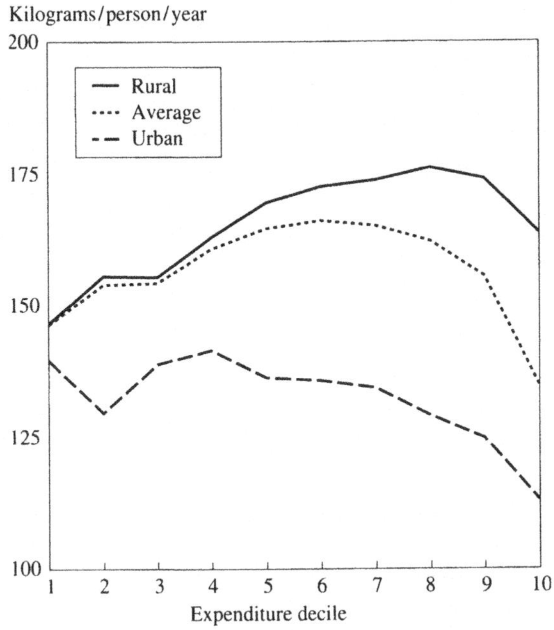

Source: Data from the Viet Nam Living Standards Survey, 1992–93.

Notes: The deciles are defined on the basis of the real value of consumption expenditure per capita, including the imputed value of home production and the rental equivalent of housing and consumer durables. All deciles are defined according to national rankings rather than within urban and rural areas.

person, P is Stone's price index, Z_k are household characteristics, and α_i, λ_{ij}, γ_i, θ_i, and δ_{ik} are parameters to be estimated. The demand equations for the food categories are estimated simultaneously in order to allow the imposition of symmetry on the cross-price substitution terms.[18]

The food system includes 14 food categories, described in Table 32. The independent variables include per capita consumption expenditure (x/P), food prices (p_j), and the following household characteristics (Z_k): household size, the proportion of adults in the household, the proportion of infants, dummy variables for urban house-

[18] Nonfood categories are not included in the demand system, largely because of the difficulty of constructing price indexes for them. In focusing on food demand, this study implicitly assumes weak separability in preferences between food and nonfood categories. Under weak separability, the utility function takes the form $U = f(v1(q1), v2(q2))$, where $v1$ and $v2$ are subutility functions and $q1$ and $q2$ are vectors of the two categories of goods. Weak separability between food and nonfood categories is a common assumption in applied demand analysis (Deaton and Muellbauer 1980, 120–133).

Table 32—Dependent variables in model of food demand

Variable	Description	Mean	Standard deviation
rice	Budget share of rice	0.2804	0.1480
mze	Budget share of maize	0.0033	0.0204
ogr	Budget share of other grain products (flour, bread, noodles)	0.0163	0.0217
cas	Budget share of cassava	0.0025	0.0116
swp	Budget share of sweet potatoes	0.0036	0.0092
leg	Budget share of legumes including beans and peanuts	0.0126	0.0153
fvg	Budget share of fruits and vegetables	0.0359	0.0233
port	Budget share of pork	0.0556	0.0441
otmt	Budget share of other meat	0.0319	0.0332
fish	Budget share of fish and seafood	0.0515	0.0508
sug	Budget share of sugar	0.0133	0.0149
oil	Budget share of cooking oil	0.0089	0.0141
ofood	Budget share of other food	0.0199	0.0229
bev	Budget share of beverages including tea, coffee, carbonated drinks, alcohol.	0.0510	0.0549

Source: Based on data from VLSS 1992–93.

holds and female-headed households, and regional dummy variables (Table 33). For the more homogeneous food groups, such as rice, maize, and cassava, the unit value of transactions carried out by the household were used for prices. For heterogenous groups, such as beverages, a price index was calculated using community prices collected as part of the VLSS.

The estimation of food demand parameters was conducted separately for the northern and southern parts of the country. The results for expenditure and own-price elasticities are reported in Table 34. The regression equations explain between 54 and 71 percent of the variation in the budget share of rice across households. This is relatively high for a cross-sectional demand equation, reflecting the fact that rice consumption is largely determined by fundamental economic factors (for example, income, prices, and household composition) rather than household-specific habits and preferences. The model is less successful in explaining variation in the budget shares of the other food categories. The R^2 for these food groups varies between 0.08 and 0.18.

The expenditure elasticities are statistically significant, particularly for the staple foods.[19] The expenditure elasticity of rice varies between 0.10 in the south and 0.48 in the north, a reflection of higher incomes in the south.[20] Maize and cassava are in-

[19] In the AIDS model, an income coefficient that is significantly different from zero implies that the expenditure elasticity is significantly different from 1.0

[20] As incomes rise, households probably also shift toward higher-quality rice, but the data do not allow us to measure this.

Table 33—Independent variables in model of food demand

Variable	Description	Mean	St. dev.
exp	Real expenditure per capita (1,000 dong/year/person)	1,458	1,047
urbexp	Interaction between urban dummy variable and ln(exp)	1.406	2.809
p_rice	Unit value of rice purchased (1,000 dong/kilogram)	1.986	0.408
p_mze	Unit value of maize purchased (1,000 dong/kilogram)	1.526	0.746
p_otg	Index of community prices of other grains (1,000 dong/kilogram)	2.753	0.884
p_cas	Unit value of cassava purchased (1,000 dong/kilogram)	0.620	0.321
p_swp	Unit value of sweet potatoes purchased (1,000 dong/kilogram)	0.767	0.352
p_leg	Index of community legume prices (1,000 dong/kilogram)	3.837	0.720
p_fvg	Index of community fruit and vegetable prices (1,000 dong/kilogram)	1.874	0.531
p_port	Unit value of pork purchased (1,000 dong/kilogram)	12.480	2.998
p_otmt	Index of community prices of other meat (1,000 dong/kilogram)	9.717	1.521
p_fish	Index of other grain prices (1,000 dong/kilogram)	9.203	3.715
p_sug	Unit value of sugar purchased (1,000 dong/kilogram)	4.774	1.539
p_oil	Unit value of oil purchased by household (1,000 dong/kilogram)	9.356	2.307
p_ofood	Index of community prices of other foods (1,000 dong/kilogram)	6.323	2.950
p_bev	Index of community prices of beverage (1,000 dong/kilogram)	10.849	1.957
hhsize	Size of household (persons)	5.000	2.150
fem	Dummy variable for female-headed households	0.267	0.443
pctad	Proportion of household members over 15 years old	0.634	0.228
pctinf	Proportion of household members under 5 years old	0.225	0.210
urb	Dummy variable for urban households	0.202	0.401
reg1	Dummy variable for households in Northern Uplands	0.167	0.373
reg2	Dummy variable for households in the Red River Delta	0.244	0.430
reg3	Dummy variable for households in the North Central Coast	0.138	0.345
reg4	Dummy variable for households in the South Central Coast	0.110	0.313
reg5	Dummy variable for households in the Central Highlands	0.027	0.161
reg6	Dummy variable for households in the Southeast	0.113	0.317

Source: Based on data from the VLSS 1992–93.

Table 34—Expenditure and price elasticities for different food categories

Food category	Expenditure elasticity North	Expenditure elasticity South	Own-price elasticity North	Own-price elasticity South
Rice	0.48[a]	0.11[a]	-0.20[a]	-0.38[a]
Maize	-1.47[a]	-0.10[a]	-4.35[a]	-1.80[a]
Grains	1.55[a]	1.55[a]	-1.22[a]	-1.17
Cassava	-0.74[a]	-1.03[a]	-1.63[a]	-2.55[a]
Sweet potatoes	0.17[a]	0.64[a]	-1.85[a]	-0.69[a]
Legumes	1.16[a]	0.92	-1.04	-1.84[a]
Fruits and vegetables	0.80[a]	1.01	-0.93	-1.01
Pork	1.17[a]	1.30[a]	-0.43[a]	-0.44[a]
Other meat	1.50[a]	1.33[a]	-1.24	-0.76
Fish	1.09[a]	1.05[a]	-1.30[a]	-1.15[a]
Sugar	1.45[a]	1.38[a]	-1.11	-0.90
Oil	1.14[a]	0.63[a]	0.23[a]	-0.61[a]
Beverage	1.28[a]	1.17[a]	-1.16[a]	-1.12[a]
Other food	1.22	1.34[a]	-1.18[a]	-1.15

Source: Econometric estimation of demand based on VLSS data.
[a]Coefficient is different from zero with a 95 percent statistical significance. In the case of the expendi- ture elasticities, this implies that the null hypothesis that the expenditure elasticity 1.0 can be rejected, that is, that budget share is constant across expenditure. In the case of the own-price elasticity, this implies that the null hypothesis that the Hicksian own-price elasticity is significantly different from –1.0 can be rejected.

ferior goods at the mean income level, while the highest elasticities are those of other grains (mainly wheat products), pork, other meats, sugar, and beverages.

The effect of own-prices on food demand is also shown in Table 34. Most of the elasticities are statistically significant.[21] The (Marshallian) own-price elasticity of rice demand varies from –0.20 in the north to –0.38 in the south, an indication of more substitutability between rice and other commodities in the latter region. The other staples are fairly price elastic, presumably due to the close substitutability with rice. Most of the other price elasticities are close to unity, except for those of pork and oil, whose demand is price-inelastic.

Tables 35 and 36 summarize the effects of household characteristics on food demand. Other things being equal, urban households consume less maize, cassava, and sweet potato, probably reflecting the fact that, for many rural households, the opportunity cost of staples is less than the market price. Urban households consume more legumes, pork, fish, and sugar. Urban areas in the north consume more rice than

[21] In the AIDS model, a significant own-price coefficient that is significantly different from zero implies that the Hicksian own-price elasticity is significantly different from B1.

Table 35—Effect of household characteristics on food demand in the north

Food	Urban area		Female-headed household		Household size		Percent adults		Percent infants	
category	Coefficient	*t*-statistic	Coefficient	*t*-statistic	Coefficient	*t*-statistic	Coefficient	*t*-statistic	Coefficient	*t*-statistic
Rice	0.35	4.84	0.001	0.32	0.001	1.085	0.046	3.674	0.062	4.907
Maize	-0.155	-7.952	0.001	0.887	0	-1.224	0.005	1.535	0.002	0.731
Grains	-0.007	-0.572	-0.001	-1.52	-0.001	-4.939	-0.008	-3.892	-0.006	-2.84
Cassava	-0.038	-3.737	0.001	0.973	0	-0.547	0.002	1.194	0.004	2.249
Sweet potato	-0.018	-2.168	0	0.204	0	2.999	0.001	0.862	0	-0.068
Legumes	0.07	5.735	0.002	2.337	0	-0.972	0	-0.239	0	-0.057
Fruits and vegetables	0.024	1.506	0.002	1.868	-0.002	-8.717	-0.003	-0.978	0.002	0.771
Pork	0.07	2.443	-0.004	-2.401	-0.002	-4.513	-0.011	-2.28	-0.006	-1.163
Other meat	-0.155	-6.179	-0.004	-2.516	-0.001	-2.216	-0.019	-4.519	-0.01	-2.306
Fish	0.041	1.474	-0.001	-0.852	0	-0.719	-0.003	-0.658	-0.008	-1.788
Sugar	0.017	1.741	-0.001	-1.09	-0.001	-3.297	-0.013	-8.022	-0.01	-6.005
Oil	0.02	2.123	0.001	1.373	0	-0.045	-0.003	-1.877	-0.001	-0.651
Beverage	-0.044	-2.381	-0.008	-6.913	0.001	2.281	-0.001	-0.202	-0.006	-1.986
Other food	-0.199	-6.031	-0.002	-0.825	-0.001	-1.068	-0.024	-4.331	-0.018	-3.137

Source: Econometric estimation of demand based on VLSS data.

Table 36—Effect of household characteristics on food demand in the south

Food	Urban area		Female headed		Household size		Percent adults		Percent infants	
category	Coefficient	*t*-statistic	Coefficient	*t*-statistic	Coefficient	*t*-statistic	Coefficient	*t*-statistic	Coefficient	*t*-statistic
Rice	-0.639	-14.521	-0.008	-2.208	-0.001	-0.989	0.076	6.617	0.055	4.552
Maize	-0.013	-2.968	0	-0.952	0	-2.411	0.001	0.609	0	0.019
Grains	0.071	4.926	0.001	0.786	0	-1.343	-0.021	-5.689	-0.009	-2.373
Cassava	-0.018	-3.618	0	-0.308	0	-1.283	0.001	0.585	0.001	0.688
Sweet potato	-0.002	-0.686	0	0.724	0	0.801	-0.001	-1.705	-0.001	-0.799
Legumes	0.029	3.76	0.002	2.294	-0.001	-4.048	0.003	1.442	0.004	1.642
Fruits and vegetables	0.068	4.692	0.002	1.585	-0.002	-7.252	-0.013	-3.447	-0.006	-1.477
Pork	0.101	3.798	0.003	1.203	-0.002	-3.709	-0.012	-1.722	-0.016	-2.111
Other meat	0.052	2.914	-0.002	-1.047	-0.001	-1.99	-0.017	-3.611	-0.016	-3.186
Fish	0.166	5.058	-0.001	-0.177	-0.001	-1.714	-0.017	-1.975	-0.005	-0.516
Sugar	0.056	5.746	0	-0.232	-0.001	-3.333	-0.023	-9.036	-0.017	-6.494
Oil	0.006	0.71	0.001	0.694	-0.001	-4.899	0.002	1.114	0.001	0.432
Beverage	0.031	2.728	-0.007	-7.339	0	-1.322	-0.001	-0.277	-0.001	-0.479
Other food	0.102	2.812	-0.008	-2.382	0	0.538	-0.016	-1.736	-0.016	-1.55

Source: Econometric estimation of demand based on VLSS data.

rural areas, whereas the opposite is true in the south. Female-headed households consume more legumes and fruits and vegetables and less beverages than other households. Larger households consume less fruits and vegetables, pork, and sugar. A large proportion of children 5 to 15 years old (the excluded category) implies less rice consumption and more sugar and meat consumption.

Calorie Consumption

The estimation of food demand parameters provides important insights on the relation between rice prices and total calorie consumption. As seen in the previous section, a 10 percent increase in rice prices results in a 2 to 4 percent decrease in rice consumption. The effect of rice price increases on caloric intake, however, is also affected by changes in the consumption of other foods. In general, higher rice prices are expected to increase the consumption of other staples, thus dampening the effect of higher rice prices on caloric intake.

The estimated food demand elasticities are used to quantify these effects. The elasticity of caloric intake with respect to income (consumption expenditure), η_c, can be calculated as follows:

$$\eta_c = \sum_{i=1}^{14} \eta_i \omega_i, \tag{3}$$

where η_i is the income elasticity of food i and ω_i is the contribution of food i to - total caloric intake. The elasticity of caloric intake with respect to rice price, ε_{cr}, is calculated as

$$\varepsilon_{cr} = \sum_{i=1}^{14} \varepsilon_{ir} \eta_i, \tag{4}$$

where ε_{ir} is the elasticity of demand for food i with respect to the price of rice.

Table 37 reports the elasticity of caloric intake with respect to income and rice prices. The calorie income elasticities imply that a 10 percent increase in income is associated with a 5 percent increase in caloric intake. The calorie-income elasticities are higher than the rice-income elasticities because, as income rises, caloric intake rises from several sources in addition to rice. As expected, calorie income elasticities are higher in the north than in the south. Because the north is poorer, a larger proportion of additional spending goes to food and to staple foods in particular, compared with the south.

The calorie-rice price elasticities suggest that a 10 percent increase in rice prices would result in a 2 percent reduction in caloric intake. The calorie-rice price elasticities are lower than the price elasticity of rice demand. The reason is that a higher rice price causes increases in demand for other foods that offset the reduction in calories from rice.

Table 37—Calorie elasticities

Elasticity	Viet Nam	North	South
Elasticity of caloric intake with respect to income	0.53	0.61	0.35
Elasticity of caloric intake with respect to rice price	-0.21	-0.18	-0.31

Source: Calculated from the estimated demand elasticities in Table 35 and caloric shares for each food category (see text).

Conclusions

The VLSS reveals that the importance of rice in Viet Nam is not limited to the delta regions. Even in the northern and central highlands, it accounts for three-quarters of the caloric intake of the average household. Per capita rice consumption is lower among urban households than rural ones. In addition, rice consumption rises with income at low- and middle-income levels, but it falls as income rises further. Using regression analysis, the study estimates that the expenditure elasticity of the rice demand is 0.38 at the mean income level, while the price elasticity is –0.24. The price and income elasticities estimated from the food demand model imply that the elasticity of caloric intake with respect to income is 0.5, while the elasticity of caloric intake with respect to the rice price is –0.2.

The relationship between income and rice demand in Asia is the subject of some debate. Using panel data for 14 Asian countries, Ito, Peterson, and Grant (1989) found that rice was an inferior good in half of them. Huang, David, and Duff (1991), however, re-estimated the elasticities using different methods and concluded that rice was inferior only in the higher-income Asian countries: Japan, Malaysia, Singapore, Taiwan, and Thailand. Huang and David (1993) noted that rice demand is constant or falling in a number of Asian countries, including Bangladesh, India, and Pakistan, but that much of this is the result of urbanization rather than income growth.

The results here are broadly consistent with these trends. Cross-sectional analysis using 1993 data finds that the income elasticity of rice demand in Viet Nam is small but positive. And the trends in apparent consumption suggest that in spite of rapid income growth, per capita rice demand has been relatively flat since 1993.

CHAPTER 5

Poverty and Rice Prices

It is clear from previous chapters that rice plays an important role in the Vietnamese economy and that the government is concerned about the impact of rice market liberalization on the poor. A key question, therefore, is what effect does a change in rice prices have on incomes and poverty in Viet Nam? As discussed in Chapter 1, higher food prices almost always have a negative effect on urban households, but the effect on rural households is ambiguous. In order to assess the overall effect on poverty, information on the distribution of poverty must be combined with information on the impact of higher rice prices on different household types.

This chapter begins with a description of the distribution of poverty in Viet Nam. Next, household data on rice production and consumption are used to calculate the short-term elasticity of real income with respect to rice prices. Finally, all of this information is combined to estimate the effect of uniform higher rice prices on the poverty rate. This analysis is extended in Chapter 6 to consider the effect of market liberalization on rice prices and hence on incomes and poverty.

Poverty in Viet Nam

The General Statistics Office (GSO) has traditionally obtained information on household living standards using journals completed by households. These journals were collected annually, aggregated by local GSO officials, and sent to GSO headquarters. Surveys of this type were used to collect information on household expenditure, income, and assets, but the sample coverage was limited to selected provinces. In 1990, GSO carried out a direct-interview survey of household production activities in five provinces (World Bank 1995).

The first nationally representative household survey using direct interviews was the 1992–93 Viet Nam Living Standards Survey (VLSS), described in Chapter 4. The World Bank carried out a poverty assessment using the VLSS data with upper and lower poverty lines. According to these calculations, 51 percent of the population lives below the upper poverty line and 41 percent lives below the lower poverty line, although there is considerable regional variation (World Bank 1995).

This section describes the incidence and depth of poverty among different groups of households based on a reanalysis of the VLSS data. The analysis here differs from that of the World Bank in two respects. First, this report excludes from the analysis 287 households whose per capita caloric intake is either too high (above 3,500 calories) or too low (below 1,000 calories) to be plausible. Since food consumption accounts for more than half of consumption expenditure, implausible caloric intake figures may suggest unreliable measurement of consumption expenditure. Household weights are used to ensure that this exclusion does not affect the importance of each region in the analysis. Second, a more restrictive, relative definition of poverty is adopted here because the focus of the analysis is on the variation in poverty across groups and in changes in poverty under different policy scenarios, rather than the level of poverty using an internationally comparable poverty line. Furthermore, for the purposes of this study, a more restrictive definition of poverty corresponds more closely to the group that policymakers would like to protect from adverse effects. Thus, the poor are defined as those in the bottom 25 percent in terms of real per capita consumption expenditure.[22]

Table 38 describes the degree of poverty in each household group using three of the poverty measures identified by Foster, Greer, and Thorbecke (1984).[23] P_0 is simply the incidence of poverty (the proportion of households falling below the poverty line). P_1 is the poverty gap index, defined as the incidence of poverty multiplied by the gap between the poverty line and the average income among the poor. P_2 is an index of the severity of poverty, taking into account not just the proportion of poor households and the average income of the poor, but the variance of income among the poor. The last three columns of Table 38 show the proportion of national poverty that each household group represents.

Table 38 highlights the fact that rural poverty is more widespread and more severe than urban poverty. In fact, the poverty rate (P_0) is almost four times higher in the rural areas than in urban areas. As a result, 94 to 96 percent of Vietnamese poverty is located in rural areas.

With regard to regional differences, the North Central Coast and the Northern Uplands have the largest proportion of poor households according to P_0, but poverty is most severe in the Central Highlands according to P_2. Being poor or heavily populated, or both, the three northern regions together account for more than two-thirds of the poverty in Viet Nam. Although poverty is most severe in the Central Highlands, its small population means that it accounts for only 2 to 5 percent of national poverty.

Farmers, who represent 74 percent of the population, have a poverty rate three times that of nonfarmers. As a result, they account for more than 90 percent of the poverty in Viet Nam. The fact that poverty is greater among farmers than among ru-

---

[22] Consumption expenditure includes the value of home-produced food, consumption purchases, and the rental value of consumer durables and owner-occupied housing. Local prices are used to value nonmarket transactions. A price index is used to adjust for differences in the cost of living across regions and between urban and rural areas.

[23] The class of measures is defined by $P_a = (1/N)\,\Sigma\,[(x-x_i)/x]^a$, where N is the total population, x is the poverty line, x_i is the income of poor household i, and the summation is limited to poor households.

Table 38—Poverty rates and distribution of poor households

Household category	Share of population	Poverty index P_0	P_1	P_2	Contribution to national poverty P_0	P_1	P_2
				(percent)			
Viet Nam	100.0	25.0	6.1	2.3	100.0	100.0	100.0
Location							
Urban	20.0	7.6	1.6	0.5	6.1	5.4	4.4
Rural	80.0	29.4	7.2	2.7	93.9	94.6	95.6
Region							
Northern Uplands	16.7	34.9	8.3	3.0	23.3	22.8	22.0
Red River Delta	24.0	25.1	6.6	2.7	24.1	26.0	28.6
Northern Central Coast	13.3	40.4	9.8	3.5	21.5	21.4	20.7
Southern Central Coast	11.3	20.0	4.9	1.8	9.0	9.1	8.9
Central Highlands	2.7	21.9	7.9	3.8	2.4	3.5	4.5
Southeast	11.3	12.1	2.6	0.9	5.5	4.8	4.3
Mekong River Delta	20.7	17.2	3.6	1.2	14.2	12.2	11.1
Occupation							
Farmer	73.7	30.7	7.5	2.8	90.4	90.8	91.9
Nonfarmer	26.3	9.1	2.1	0.7	9.5	9.2	8.1

Source: Data from the Viet Nam Living Standards Survey.

Notes: Poverty is defined as households below the 25th percentile in terms of per capita consumption expenditure. P_0, P_1, and P_2 refer to three of the poverty measures in the class identified by Foster, Greer, and Thorbecke (1984). P_0 is the incidence of poverty, P_1 is the poverty gap index, and P_2 is the index of the severity of poverty.

ral households in general implies that nonfarm rural households tend to be better off than farming rural households.

A more detailed picture of the geographic distribution of rural poverty can be obtained by combining information from the VLSS with district level data from the 1994 Agricultural Census. First, the VLSS data are used to estimate the probability that a household is poor as a function of 19 household characteristics and 6 regional dummy variables. The household characteristics include household size and composition, farm size, food production, proportion of land in perennial crops, ownership of different types of livestock, size and building material of house, type of water supply, and ownership of radios, televisions, and motorbikes. Next, the district-level average values are compiled for these same 19 indicators and dummy variables from the 1994 Agricultural Census. Finally, these district-level values are inserted into the poverty equation obtained in the first step. This gives a poverty indicator at the district level that can be mapped using geographic information system (GIS) software (Minot 1998; Minot 2000).

Figure 7—Geographic distribution of poverty

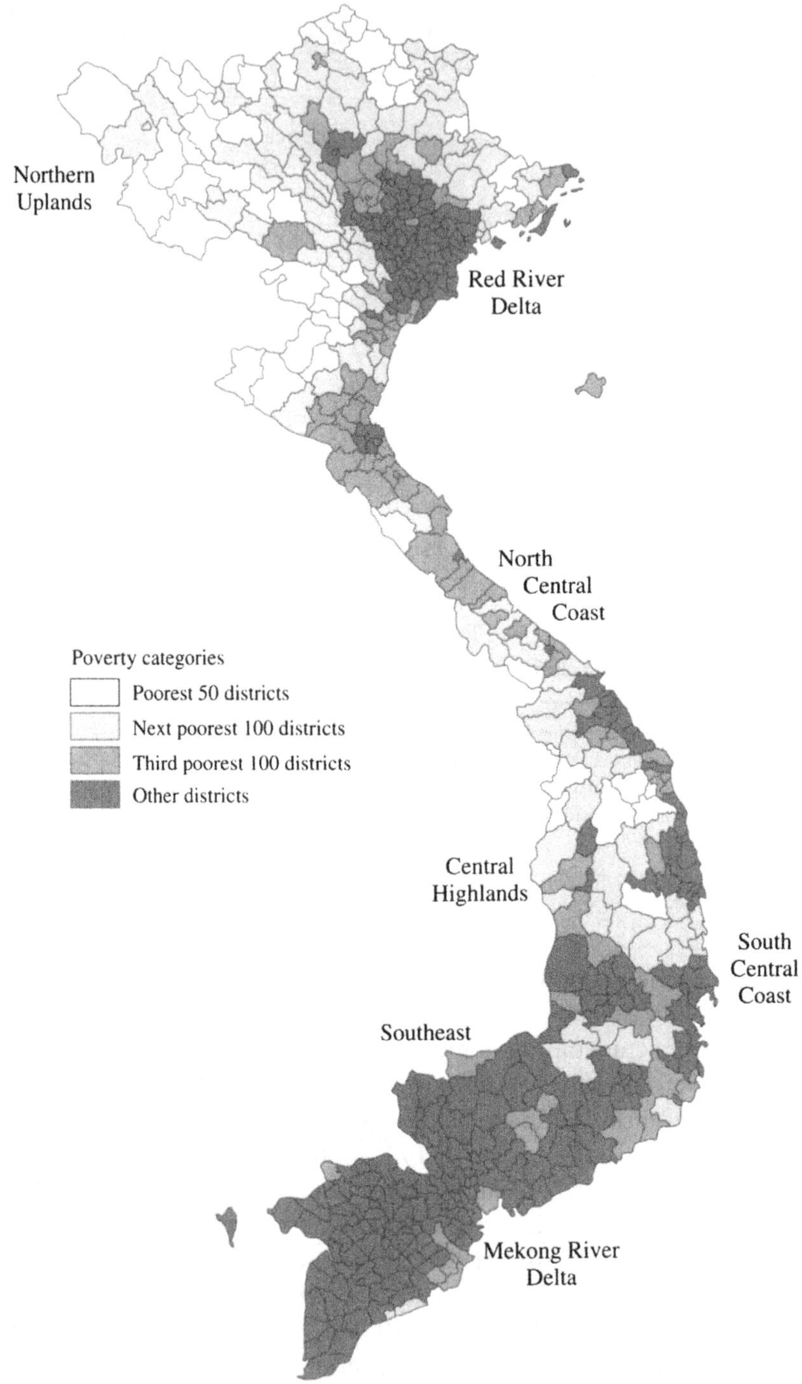

The results of this analysis are presented in Figure 7. More than half of the poorest 50 districts are concentrated along the northern and western edges of the Northern Uplands. These are remote mountainous regions with large ethnic minority populations. Other pockets of poverty can be found in the northwestern section of the North Central Coast and the northern part of the Central Highlands. None of the poorest 50 districts is on the coast, and none are in the deltas or in the Southeast. The darkest shade represents the least poor districts. Almost all the districts in the Mekong, the Red River Delta, and the Southeast fall into this category.

Rice Marketing Patterns and Household Welfare

The direct welfare effect of higher food prices on a household depends on its net sales position, as noted by Mellor (1978). Households who are net sellers, such as commercial farmers, gain from higher prices, while those who are net buyers, such as urban consumers and landless rural households, lose.[24] Mellor's data from India revealed that only the poorest quintile of rural households were net buyers.

Other studies show a surprisingly high proportion of net food buyers among rural households in developing countries. Weber et al. (1988) reviewed the results from five studies in Sub-Saharan Africa, showing that 15 to 73 percent of farm households are net buyers, depending on the crop and the country. Barrett and Dorosh (1996) estimate that net buyers of rice account for 49 percent of the farmers in Madagascar, while Sahn (1998) finds that 84 percent of the rural households in Sri Lanka are net buyers of rice. A study of Thailand found that net buyers of rice represented 58 percent of rural households and 25 percent of rice farmers (Trairatvorakul 1984).

A number of studies have quantified the welfare impact of food price changes. Computable general equilibrium models have been widely used to examine the impact of policy on different household groups (for example, see Bourguignon, de Melo, and Morrison 1991). These models are comprehensive in tracing the effects of policy on land, labor, and capital markets, as well as interaction between agricultural and nonagricultural sectors. However, they often do not provide the distributional detail of partial equilibrium approaches.

Trairatvorakul (1984) estimates the effect of rice price increases on the poverty rate and caloric intake. Deaton (1989) combines household data and hypothesized price changes to study the distributional effect of higher rice prices in Thailand. Similar methods were adopted in studies of the distributional effect of higher food prices in Côte d'Ivoire (Budd 1993) and in Madagascar (Barrett and Dorosh 1996).

Deaton (1989) highlights the importance of the net benefit ratio (NBR), defined as the value of net sales of a commodity as a proportion of income. The NBR for a commodity can be interpreted as the "before-response" or "impact" elasticity of real income with respect to the price of that commodity. The NBR is a very short-term

[24] This reasoning applies only to the direct effect of prices on households. Households may also be affected by indirect effects, such as changes in the labor market or changes in the demand for nonfarm goods and services.

measure in that it assumes no response from households as producers or as consumers. Furthermore, it assumes no change in labor markets or nonfarm income that might result from the price change.

The VLSS provides detailed information on the patterns of rice consumption and production for different types of households. Table 39 gives the budget share of rice (the value of rice consumption as a percentage of consumption expenditure), the income share of rice (the value of rice production as a percentage of consumption expenditure), and the NBR for rice (the income share minus the budget share). On average, rice production is equivalent to 31.5 percent of household income, while the mean budget share of rice is 29.6 percent. The NBR is 1.9 percent (31.5 to 29.6). Thus, a 10 percent increase in farmgate and retail rice prices would raise real income 0.19 percent, on average.

Among urban households, rice production is minimal (3.3 percent of income), while rice consumption represents 17 percent of income. The negative NBR for urban households implies that they are net buyers and will lose from higher rice prices. Among rural households, rice production and rice consumption are much larger relative to income, and the NBR is positive, implying that rural households are net sellers and will, on average, gain from higher rice prices. For a given price increase, the loss for the average urban household is more than twice as large as the gain for the average rural household.

Turning to regional patterns, the importance of rice in household incomes is highest in the Red River Delta (42 percent) and the Mekong River Delta (38 percent) and lowest in the urbanized Southeast (14 percent). The budget share of rice ranges from almost 35 percent in the two northernmost regions to just 19 percent in the Southeast. This pattern reflects regional variation in income: the northern regions tend to be poorer, while the Southeast (which includes Ho Chi Minh City) has the highest average income. The NBR is negative in the five rice-deficit regions, and positive in the two delta regions. The overall positive NBR is explained by the fact that the two delta regions account for 45 percent of the population. Futhermore, the absolute value of the positive NBRs in the deltas is larger than that of the negative NBRs in the deficit regions.

Rice marketing patterns naturally vary widely between farmers and nonfarmers. Among farmers, one-third of their income is allocated to rice, but rice production represents 42 percent of income, resulting in a positive NBR. Nonfarmers have much smaller rice budget shares (reflecting their higher income), but negligible production, yielding a negative NBR.[25]

Table 39 also reveals that the budget share of rice falls from 45 percent for the poorest quartile to 13 percent for the richest. The importance of rice production relative to income also falls with higher income. Although rich rice farmers produce and sell larger amounts of rice than poor rice farmers, rich households are less likely to be rice farmers in the first place. The NBR does not show a consistent pattern, with

---

[25] Farmers and nonfarmers are defined according to the most important source of income. Thus, under this definition, a nonfarmer may have some agricultural production and income.

Table 39—Rice production, consumption, and net sales by household group

Household category	Rice production as percent of income (PR)	Rice consumption as percent of income (CR)	Net sales of rice as percent of income (NBR)	Net sellers of rice	Zero net position in rice	Net buyers of rice
	(average percentage)			(percent of households)		
Viet Nam	31.5	29.6	1.9	32.4	7.2	60.4
Location						
Urban	3.3	17.1	-13.8	4.1	1.0	94.9
Rural	38.5	32.7	5.8	39.5	8.7	51.8
Region						
Northern Uplands	28.8	34.8	-6.0	24.1	14.1	61.8
Red River Delta	42.5	34.8	7.7	45.9	8.7	45.4
North Central Coast	32.6	33.9	-1.3	31.7	9.5	58.8
South Central Coast	19.3	25.6	-6.3	18.4	5.7	75.9
Central Highlands	19.3	32.6	-13.4	10.0	7.5	82.5
Southeast	14.3	19.0	-4.8	16.6	2.3	81.0
Mekong River Delta	37.8	24.3	13.6	43.1	1.1	55.2
Occupation						
Farmer	42.5	33.7	8.8	44.0	9.4	46.6
Nonfarmer	0.5	18.2	-17.7	0.0	0.8	99.2
Income group						
1st (poorest) quartile	47.5	45.5	2.1	38.8	10.8	50.4
2nd quartile	34.8	34.5	0.2	33.8	6.6	59.5
3rd quartile	27.8	25.1	2.7	32.2	6.6	61.3
4th quartile	15.9	13.3	2.5	24.9	4.7	70.4

Source: Calculated from data from the Viet Nam Living Standards Survey (1992–93).
Notes: PR is the production ratio, CR is the consumption ratio, and NBR is the net benefit ratio.

the second quartile appearing to gain less from rice price increases than the other quartiles.

The last three columns of Table 39 show the percentage of households that are net sellers (NBR > 0), that have no net sales (NBR = 0), and that are net buyers (NBR < 0). Overall, less than one-third of Vietnamese households are net sellers who would gain in the short run from higher rice prices.[26] Less than 40 percent of *rural*

[26] As noted earlier, the production figures were adjusted to reflect the 12 percent increase in rice output between the 1992–93 VLSS survey and the calibration year (1995). Information is not available on how this increase was distributed among households, so it is assumed that the proportion of net sellers did not change. To the extent that the number of surplus rice farmers increased between 1992–93 and 1995, the proportion of net sellers will be underestimated.

households have net rice sales and somewhat more than half are net buyers. The proportion of net sellers is, as expected, highest in the two delta regions, but even in these two regions net sellers account for less than half of the households. Finally, the proportion of net sellers is higher among low-income groups than among high-income groups, though even in the lowest quartile surplus households make up less than 40 percent of the total.

Overall, it is notable that the proportion of households with zero net position in rice markets is small. More than 90 percent of rural households have some interaction with rice markets, either as buyers or as sellers. The proportion of households with zero net sales rises from barely 1 percent in the Mekong to 14 percent in the Northern Uplands, reflecting the increasing degree of orientation to subsistence farming as one moves north. Furthermore, poor households are twice as likely as rich ones to not participate in the market at all. This may be because the poor are often farmers in remote areas with high transaction costs, or it may be related to risk aversion among poor households.

In summary, 6 out of 10 households and 5 out of 7 regions are net buyers of rice, implying that a majority would lose from higher rice prices in the short run. The region that would gain the most, the Mekong River Delta, is one of the richest, while the region that would lose the most, the Central Highlands, is one of the poorest. As shown later, the actual distributional effect of higher rice prices is less negative than suggested by these figures.

Rice Prices and Poverty

The previous section examined the rice marketing patterns to determine which groups of households would lose and which would gain from an increase in rice prices. In this section, household-level marketing data from the VLSS are used to estimate the impact of a uniform 10 percent increase in rice prices on real income and poverty. Two expressions are used for the real income effect, one for the "before-response" effect and another for the "after-response" effect. The before-response effect refers to the effect in the very short term, before producers and consumers respond to the price change. The after-response effect refers to the effect after they respond to the new prices[27] (the derivation of these equations is given in Appendix 2). The before-response welfare effect of changes in rice prices is given by

$$\frac{\Delta w_i^1}{x_{0i}} = \frac{\Delta p_r^p}{p_{0r}^p} PR_{ir} - \frac{\Delta p_r^c}{p_{0r}^c} CR_{ir} \tag{5}$$

where Δw_i^1 = the first-order approximation of the change in welfare for household i of a change in rice price,

[27] The after-response welfare effect could describe either short- or long-term effects, depending on the type of elasticities used.

x_{0i} = original income (consumption expenditure) of household i,

p_{0r}^{p} = the original value of the price used to value rice production in region r;

p_{0r}^{c} = the original value of the price used to value rice consumption in region r;

PR_{ir} = the value of rice production for household i as a proportion of x_{0i}, and

CR_{ir} = the value of rice consumption for household i as a proportion of x_{0i}.

The after-response income effect is calculated using:

$$\frac{\Delta w_i^2}{x_{0i}} = \frac{\Delta p_r^p}{p_{0r}^p} PR_{ir} + \frac{1}{2}\left(\frac{\Delta p_r^p}{p_{0r}^p}\right)^2 PR_{ir}\, \varepsilon_{rr}^{s} - \frac{\Delta p_r^c}{p_{0r}^c} CR_{ir} - \frac{1}{2}\left(\frac{\Delta p_r^c}{p_{0r}^c}\right)^2 CR_{ir}\, \varepsilon_{rr}^{H}, \tag{6}$$

where Δw_i^2 = the second-order approximation of the change in welfare for household i of a change in rice price,

ε_{rr}^{S} = the own-price elasticity of rice supply, and

ε_{rr}^{H} = the own-price Hicksian elasticity of rice demand.

These expressions are extensions of the NBR used to study the distributional impact of food price changes in several studies (Deaton 1989; Budd 1993; and Barrett and Dorosh 1996). Equation (5) is similar to the NBR calculation except that it allows the percentage change in producer prices to differ from that of consumer prices. Equation (6) is like equation (5), except that it includes terms to represent the response of consumers and producers to the price changes. If the elasticities in equation (6) are set at zero and the percentage changes in producer and consumer prices are equal to each other, this expression collapses to the NBR used in previous studies.

The values of PR_{ir} and CR_{ir} are based on the 1992–93 VLSS, with adjustments to reflect the 12 percent increase in rice production between the survey and the calibration year (1995). The supply elasticities are based on an econometric analysis of time-series data by Khiem and Pingali (1995), while the demand elasticities are based on the demand analysis described in Chapter 4.

The first column of Table 40 shows the before-response effect of a 10 percent increase in rice prices on the real income of different household groups. Because the producer and consumer prices are both assumed to increase by the same 10 percent, the first column is simply the NBR (= PR – CR) multiplied by the proportional price increase (0.1). Rural households, residents of the two delta regions, and farmers gain from the increase in rice prices. But nonfarmers, urban households, and residents of the five deficit regions lose. The net effect is a small positive effect, indicating that the average income of Vietnamese households rises.

Table 40—Effect of a 10 percent increase in rice prices by household group

Household category	Average change in real income: Impact	Average change in real income: Short-term	Poverty rate: Before impact	Poverty rate: After impact	Poverty rate: After short-term
	(percent)			(percent)	
Viet Nam	0.2	0.3	25.0	25.3	25.2
Location					
Urban	-1.4	-1.4	7.6	8.6	8.6
Rural	0.6	0.7	29.4	29.4	29.4
Region					
Northern Uplands	-0.6	-0.5	34.9	35.5	35.5
Red River Delta	0.8	0.9	25.1	24.6	24.6
North Central Coast	-0.1	-0.1	40.4	41.7	41.5
South Central Coast	-0.6	-0.5	20.0	20.5	20.5
Central Highlands	-1.3	-1.2	21.9	22.7	22.7
Southeast	-0.5	-0.4	12.1	12.9	12.9
Mekong River Delta	1.4	1.5	17.2	16.9	16.9
Occupation					
Farmer	0.9	1.0	30.7	30.5	30.5
Nonfarmer	-1.8	-1.7	9.1	10.5	10.5
Income group					
1st (poorest) quartile	0.2	0.3	100.0	96.8	96.8
2nd quartile	0.0	0.1	0.0	4.2	4.2
3rd quartile	0.3	0.3	0.0	0.0	0.0
4th quartile	0.3	0.3	0.0	0.0	0.0

Source: Household-level simulations based on data from the Viet Nam Living Standards Survey, 1992–93.

The second column gives the after-response effects of the rice price increase on Vietnamese households. In all cases, the after-response effects are somewhat more positive than the before-response effects. This result reflects the general rule that the welfare effects of a price change are more positive when consumer and producer responses are incorporated. However, the differences between short- and long-term effects are small, around 0.1 percentage points, as a result of the relatively inelastic demand and supply.

The last three columns give the incidence of poverty (P_0) before and after the 10 percent increase in rice prices. The effect of the rice price change on the poverty rate is estimated by adjusting the real income of each household in the sample and calculating the proportion of households whose new income falls below the original poverty line. Not surprisingly, the urban poverty rate rises one percentage point, as do poverty rates in the five deficit regions. Poverty rates fall in the two surplus delta regions. The net effect is a small increase in the national poverty rate, from 25.0 to 25.2 percent in the long term.

It should be emphasized that these calculations do not incorporate general equilibrium effects. In particular, they do not take into account the effects of higher rice prices on the demand for labor and wage rates, which affect household income. Since rice production is likely to be more labor-intensive than many alternative economic activities, higher rice prices would be expected to increase the demand for labor and wage rates. To the extent that the poor obtain a significant share of their income from agricultural labor, this would strengthen the poverty-reducing effect of higher rice prices. This was found to be a significant factor in a general equilibrium analysis of Thai rice prices (Warr 1997). As discussed in Chapter 2, however, landlessness and the use of hired labor are less common in Viet Nam, so the effect of rice prices on income via wage rates is likely to be weaker.

Conclusions

Viet Nam is a poor country in which 80 percent of the population lives in the rural areas. However, poverty is not evenly distributed throughout the country. Poverty is almost four times as widespread and five times as severe in the rural areas as in the urban areas. Furthermore, poverty tends to be concentrated in the more remote, hilly regions, namely the North Central Coast, the Northern Uplands, and the Central Highlands.

The effect of rice price changes on household welfare depends on the net sales position of the household: net sellers of rice will benefit from higher prices while net buyers will lose. Household survey data suggest that the two delta regions, with 45 percent of the population, are surplus regions that would gain from higher rice prices, while the other five regions are rice-deficit areas that would lose on average. Higher prices would also benefit the average rural household at the expense of urban households.

A uniform 10 percent increase in rice prices would hurt urban households, nonfarmers, and residents of the five deficit regions, although the effect on real income would be less than 2 percent on average. The price increase would benefit farmers in general, particularly those in the Red River Delta and the Mekong Delta. Average income in Viet Nam would rise by 0.3 percent on average in the long run. Somewhat paradoxically, in spite of the higher average income, the poverty rate would rise slightly from 25.0 to 25.2 percent in the long run. Overall, it is surprising that although only one-third of Vietnamese households are net sellers of rice, higher rice prices have virtually no effect on the incidence of poverty. This suggests that many of the poor are rural farmers who either (1) have net sales of rice, (2) are self-sufficient in rice, or (3) purchase such small quantities that higher rice prices have negligible effects on them.

The effect of a specific policy, such as export liberalization, will differ from the results presented here for two reasons. First, the change in rice prices will not be uniform across regions. Second, the percentage change in producer and consumer prices will not be the same. In the next chapter, the analysis is extended to simulate the effects of policy changes on rice prices in each region and the resulting effects on income and poverty among different household groups.

CHAPTER 6

Impact of Further Liberalization of Rice Markets

Viet Nam no longer faces the threat of general food shortages that plagued the country in the 1980s. As a food exporter, however, it faces new policy issues, most notably the trade-off between maintaining low prices for domestic consumers and generating foreign exchange from rice exports. In an effort to ensure domestic food security, the government imposes a binding quota on rice exports. In addition, there have been restrictions on the movement of rice within the country, partly in order to control the smuggling of rice into China.

In this chapter, a spatial equilibrium model of food markets in Viet Nam is used to examine the effects of adopting alternative policies regarding rice exports and internal rice trade, concentrating, in particular, on the effects of alternative rice export policies and the effect of the restrictions on internal trade. The distributional consequences of these policies are examined by linking the results of the model to household data on rice consumption and production patterns. Finally, a brief epilogue examines the initial impact of rice market reforms undertaken in the wake of this study.

Methods

Description of the Model

The Viet Nam Agricultural Spatial Equilibrium Model (VASEM) simulates the markets for four staple foods in seven regions of the country. The four commodities are rice, maize, sweet potatoes, and cassava, although the results presented here focus on rice, which is by far the most important staple in Viet Nam. The regions are the seven agroclimatic zones illustrated in Figure 1 on page 10.

The supply of each crop in each region is determined by the producer prices of all four commodities in that region using double-log supply functions and the short- and long-run own-price elasticities estimated econometrically by Khiem and Pingali (1995). Demand is a function of the consumer prices, per capita expenditure, and a price index, using a linear approximation of the Almost Ideal Demand System (Deaton

Table 41—Elasticities of supply of and demand for rice used in the model

Region	Income elasticity of rice demand	Marshallian own-price elasticity of rice demand	Own-price elasticity of rice supply: Short-run	Own-price elasticity of rice supply: Long-run
Northern Uplands	0.51	-0.23	0.38	0.41
Red River Delta	0.48	-0.19	0.38	0.41
North Central Coast	0.49	-0.19	0.38	0.41
South Central Coast	0.17	-0.41	0.31	0.35
Central Highlands	0.39	-0.51	0.31	0.35
Southeast	-0.05	-0.28	0.31	0.35
Mekong River Delta	0.11	-0.39	0.31	0.35
National average	0.31	-0.29	0.34	0.37

Source: Supply elasticities derived from Khiem and Pingali (1995). Demand elasticities from regression analysis of household data from the Viet Nam Living Standards Survey (1992–93) (see Chapter 4 for method used).

Note: The national averages of the demand elasticities are calculated as the consumption-weighted means of the regional elasticities, while the national averages of the supply elasticities are calculated as the production-weighted means of the regional elasticities.

and Muellbauer 1980). The demand parameters are those estimated econometrically in Chapter 4. Key supply and demand elasticities are shown in Table 41.

Markets in the model follow the rules of spatial arbitrage: trade between two regions occurs when the price difference between them reaches the transfer cost (the full cost of transporting and marketing goods from one region to the other). The price difference between two regions can equal the transfer cost (in which case there is trade between the two) or be less than the transfer costs (in which case, there is no trade between the two). This transfer cost is the estimated cost of transportation and marketing based on the results of the IFPRI survey of traders or the observed price difference between the two markets, whichever is greater. Commodities are imported when the wholesale price in a region rises as high as the import parity price for that region and exported when it falls as low as the region's export parity price.

Because Viet Nam accounts for 9 to 17 percent of world rice exports, the "large country" assumption is used and world rice prices are made endogenous. In the absence of estimates of the export demand elasticity for Vietnamese rice, the export demand elasticity for Thai rice is adopted, which is implicit in the model of world trade developed by Tyers and Anderson (1988). After adjusting for differences in the relative size of rice exports, the short-term export demand elasticity for Vietnamese rice is –15, while the long-term elasticity is –30 (see Appendix 3 for more details).

The model is calibrated to reflect Vietnamese food markets in 1995. It is solved using mixed complementarity programming (MCP) with the General Algebraic Modeling System (GAMS) software. MCP offers numerous advantages over the quadratic programming approach pioneered by Takayama and Judge (1970): supply and demand functions can be nonlinear, income effects can be incorporated into the demand equation, and quantitative restrictions can be imposed on trade (see Rutherford 1995). Appendix 4 contains the equations in the model.

Distributional Effects

The model simulates the impact of policy on supply, demand, prices, and income in each region, but it does not tell us how the policy affects different types of households within each region. The distributional effects of alternative policies are simulated by combining the regional producer and consumer rice prices from the model with household data on rice production and consumption patterns. Equation 6, described in Chapter 5, is used to estimate the welfare impact of changes in rice prices on different types of households.

Base Scenario

In the base scenario (reflecting the situation in 1995), the Mekong River Delta produces rice surpluses of 4.5 million tons, of which 2.0 million tons are shipped to other regions in the country and 2.5 million tons are exported. The export quota in 1995 was just 2.0 million tons, but large volumes of rice were smuggled into China. Both informal estimates and food balance estimates indicate that informal exports were about 0.5 million tons. The only other surplus region is the Red River Delta which supplies 190,000 tons of rice to the Northern Uplands.

Rice prices reflect these internal trade flows. Rice prices are lowest in the Mekong Delta and progressively higher as one moves north. In the Mekong, the retail price of rice is D2,345 per kilogram, or US$213 per ton, while in the Northern Uplands it is D3,220 per kilogram, or US$293 per ton. By comparison, the average f.o.b. price of Vietnamese rice exports in 1995 was US$269. The gap between the Mekong price and the border price is the result of the rice export quota, as discussed in the next section.

Rice Export Policy

This section examines the effects of alternative rice export policies on rice markets, income, and income distribution using VASEM. Alternative policies include eliminating the rice export quota, adjusting the level of the quota, and replacing the quota with an export tax. The model can be used to simulate the short-run impact (after one year) or the long-run impact (after full adjustment), depending on which parameters are used for domestic supply and international rice demand. The results of these simulations are compared to the base scenario, designed to simulate conditions in 1995 with the rice export quota.

Figure 8—Effect of an export quota (large-country assumption)

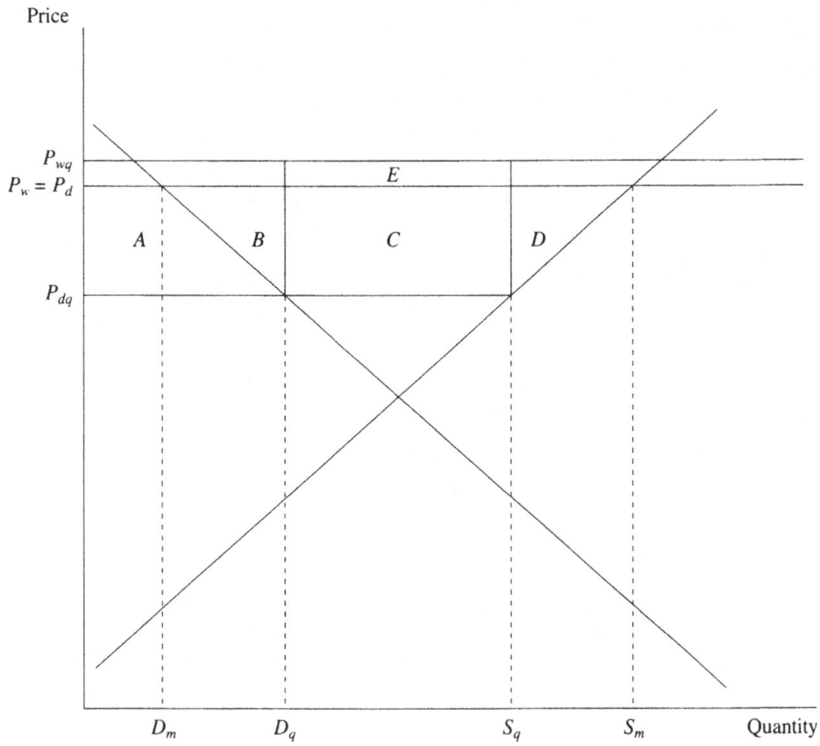

Eliminating the Rice Export Quota

A binding export quota reduces the domestic price of the commodity by reducing the demand as perceived by producers. The qualitative impact of an export quota is illustrated in Figure 8. The world price and the domestic price without the export quota are represented by $Pw = Pd$. At this price, domestic demand is D_m and supply is S_m, so exports are $S_m - D_m$. When an export quota equal to $S_q - D_q$ is imposed, the domestic price falls to P_{dq}. If the country is "large" in the market for this good, the reduction in exports will increase the world price to P_{wq}. The gap between the world price (P_{wq}) and domestic price (P_{dq}) under the quota is the implicit tax imposed by the export restrictions.

The benefits to consumers from the lower price associated with the export quota is represented by area *A*,[28] while the cost to producers is represented by $A + B + C + D$. Thus, when the quota is imposed, there is a net loss to producers and consumers

[28] To be more precise, the cost to consumers is the area behind the Hicksian, or compensated, demand curve, as shown in the derivation of the welfare measure in Appendix 4. The difference between the two is small in most cases.

of $B + C + D$. At the same time, the exporters who are given export permits[29] earn quota rents equal to the volume of exports multiplied by the gap between the domestic price and the higher world price, equivalent to area $C + E$. The net loss to the country as a whole from imposing the export quota is $B + D - E$, where $B + D$ represents the deadweight loss and E represents the terms-of-trade gain.

If the country is "small," the reduction in its exports does not affect the world price, so there is no terms-of-trade effect ($E = 0$). Thus, any export quota reduces national income. For a "large" country, it is possible for the terms-of-trade effects of a quota to be larger than the deadweight loss ($E > B + D$), implying that the country gains from the quota. This is more likely when the foreign demand for the export good is relatively inelastic and when the implicit tax associated with the quota is small.[30] These issues are discussed further in the context of the policy simulations.

The model indicates that the export quota is equivalent to a US$60 per ton tax on rice exports.[31] Since the with-quota world price (P_{wq}) is US$269, the export quota has the same effect on prices, production, and consumption as a 22 percent export tax (60/269 = 0.22). It also implies that the quota rents have a value of US$150 million (2.5 million tons at US$60 per ton).

Table 42 summarizes the impact of removing the export quota in the short and long runs. The short-run simulation uses supply elasticities and international demand elasticities that represent the effect within one year. In the short run, eliminating the rice export quota would raise the average consumer price of rice 20 percent, reducing rice consumption 4 percent and expanding rice production almost 7 percent, compared with the base scenario. These changes in production and consumption allow exports to rise from 2.5 to 3.9 million tons. Because Viet Nam is a "large country" in rice markets, export liberalization reduces the world price by 3.7 percent. This large-country effect reduces the gains to export liberalization and dampens the increase in domestic prices.

The short-run increase in household income, which refers to the effect of food prices on consumers and producers (area $B + C + D$), is US$178 million or 1.3 percent. The increase in total income, which includes changes in household income and changes in quota rents ($B + D - E$), is US$28 million. These estimates do not include the indirect, or general equilibrium, effects of the quota removal such as those related to changes in wages or nonfarm income.

The quota rent, which was US$150 million in the base scenario, disappears when

[29] Exporters may have to pay for the export permits, either formally to the government or informally to the government officials who allocate the permits. In this case, exporters share the quota rents with the government or government officials.

[30] The country is also more likely to gain from export restrictions (such as a quota) if domestic supply and demand are relatively elastic and if exports are small relative to domestic production.

[31] In mixed complementarity programming, every inequality constraint is associated with a complementary variable that indicates the shadow price of the constraint. The complementary variable associated with the export quota is the export tax equivalent (in absolute terms) of the quota.

Table 42—Overall effects of eliminating the rice export quota

			Eliminate rice export quota			
			Short-run		Long-run	
Variable	Unit	Base scenario	Level	Percent change	Level	Percent change
Rice price	Dong/kg	2,781	3,345	20.3	3,391	22.0
Paddy price	Dong/kg	1,503	1,863	24.0	1,892	25.9
Paddy production	1,000 tons	24,949	26,640	6.8	26,969	8.1
Rice production	1,000 tons	13,865	14,805	6.8	14,988	8.1
Rice consumption	1,000 tons	11,333	10,881	-4.0	10,848	-4.3
Rice exports	1,000 tons	2,532	3,924	55.0	4,139	63.5
Rice export price	US$/ton	269	259	-3.7	263	-2.1
Rice export value	US$million	681	1,016	49.3	1,089	60.0
Household income	US$million/year	13,567	13,745	1.3	13,769	1.5
Total income	US$million/year	13,716	13,745	0.2	13,769	0.4
Price index	base=100	100	104	4.6	105	5.0

Source: Simulation using the Viet Nam Agricultural Spatial Equilibrium Model.

the quota is eliminated. Most of the quota rent (US$125 million) is transferred to producers (area *C* in Figure 8), but some (US$25 million) is transferred to foreign buyers in the form of lower world prices (area *E* in Figure 8).

The long-run effects of quota removal are more favorable in terms of exports, output, and income, as shown in the last two columns of Table 42. After producers adjust fully to the higher prices, rice output expands 8 percent and exports rise to 4.1 million tons. In addition, the foreign demand for Vietnamese rice exports is more elastic in the long run, since the lower world price gradually induces other exporting countries to scale back and rice buyers to expand imports. Thus, the world price rebounds partially, ending up 2.1 percent below the base scenario, compared with 3.7 percent below in the short run. Because the world price is slightly higher in the long run than in the short, domestic rice prices are also slightly higher.

In the long run, household income rises US$202 million, while total income increases US$52 million. The gains are higher than in the short run partly because Vietnamese rice producers have time to adjust fully to the higher prices, but mostly because world demand is more elastic in the long run.[32] In the long run, only US$17

[32] As shown in Table 41, the difference between the short- and long-run supply elasticities as estimated by Khiem and Pingali (1994) is fairly small. In the sensitivity analysis, the effect of assuming a more elastic supply of rice on the quota removal simulation is described.

Table 43—Regional effects of eliminating the rice export quota

Region	Rice price	Rice production	Rice consumption	Rice surplus
	(dong/kilogram)		(1,000 metric tons)	
Levels with no-quota simulation				
Northern Uplands	3,820	1,329	1,952	-623
Red River Delta	3,579	2,811	2,522	389
North Central Coast	3,635	1,300	1,495	-195
South Central Coast	3,310	1,039	1,047	-8
Central Highlands	3,257	258	446	-188
Southeast	2,993	561	1,086	-526
Mekong River Delta	2,946	7,692	2,400	5292
Change from base scenario (with quota)			(percent)	
Northern Uplands	18.6	7.2	-1.7	-16.4
Red River Delta	20.2	8.2	-0.9	152.3
North Central Coast	19.8	8.0	-1.1	36.6
South Central Coast	22.2	6.7	-7.4	94.7
Central Highlands	22.6	6.6	-9.3	25.9
Southeast	25.1	8.2	-7.1	19.3
Mekong River Delta	25.6	8.5	-7.7	17.8

Source: Simulation using the Viet Nam Agricultural Spatial Equilibrium Model with long-run parameters.

million of the US$150 million in quota rents is transferred to foreign buyers, while the remaining US$133 million is transferred to domestic farmers.

Table 43 demonstrates that the long-run impact of the quota removal has a strong regional dimension: the percentage changes in production, consumption, and rice prices are substantially larger in the south than in the north. For example, consumer rice prices rise 25 to 26 percent in the two southern regions, 22 to 23 percent in the next two regions to the north, and 19 to 20 percent in the northern three regions. This pattern is the result of rice prices that were initially higher in the north, so that a given absolute increase in the rice price is a smaller percentage change.

Two points can be made regarding Table 43. First, price shocks in the Mekong are not fully transmitted (in percentage terms) to the "interior" regions.[33] Although partial transmission of price shocks is often attributed to trade barriers or inefficient mar-

[33] In some simulations using more elastic supply and demand, even the absolute increase is smaller in the Red River Delta and the Northern Uplands because the higher prices cause these two regions to become jointly self-sufficient in rice, thus partially "disconnecting" their prices from those in the Mekong Delta.

kets, this example demonstrates that distance and transportation costs alone can generate this phenomenon.

Second, the "interior" regions, in this context, should be defined according to the commodity flows rather than geography. The Red River Delta is a surplus region with a major port (Haiphong), yet its rice prices are partially insulated from world prices and from trade policy because it does not export and because it is some distance from the exporting region.

As mentioned in the previous section, the impact of quota removal on different types of households can be measured by combining the price changes from the model with household data on rice production and consumption. Because the welfare effect is calculated based on changes in rice prices on producers and consumers, the results do not incorporate the indirect effects of changes in other food prices, wages, and nonfarm income. In addition, the effect of the loss of quota rents is not included. The direct effect of higher rice prices is expected to be the largest and possibly the most adverse, yielding a conservative estimate of the gains from export liberalization.

The first three columns of Table 44 show the average percentage change in real income resulting from the elimination of the rice export quota. The real income of Vietnamese households rises 1.5 percent on average, while that of poor households (defined as the poorest 25 percent) rises 1.7 percent.

The real income of urban households, primarily net buyers, falls 2.8 percent as a result of the higher prices associated with eliminating the export quota. The loss is twice as great among the urban poor (–5.4 percent) than among the urban nonpoor (–2.6 percent) because rice accounts for a larger share of their expenditures. Rural households, being net sellers on average, gain from the quota removal. The rural nonpoor gain somewhat more (2.7 percent) than the rural poor (2.1 percent). This is because the farmers that produce enough rice to be net sellers are somewhat less likely to be poor than net buyers. For example, the Mekong Delta has a high proportion of net sellers (46 percent) and a small percentage of poor households (17 percent).

These results present an apparent paradox: on the one hand, poor households do less well than nonpoor households in both rural and urban areas; on the other hand, overall, poor households do better than nonpoor households. The explanation is that redistribution *between* sectors, from the richer urban sector to the poorer rural sector, is progressive and outweighs regressive distribution patterns within each sector.

Looking at the regional impact on income and poverty, the gains are largest in the two rice-surplus regions. In the Mekong and Red River deltas, average real incomes rise 5.6 and 2.4 percent, respectively. The largest loss is in the Central Highlands, where average income falls 2.4 percent. In the other regions, there is a mixture of small gains and small losses (ranging from –0.8 to 0.4 percent). Poor households generally do better than their nonpoor neighbors in the same region. This pattern is most notable in the Red River Delta where the nonpoor include the residents of Hanoi, who are hurt by higher rice prices, while the poor are mostly rice farmers. An exception to this pattern is the Mekong River Delta, where the gains by the poor are large but not as large as those of nonpoor households. The Mekong Delta is pre-

Table 44—Distributional effects of eliminating the rice export quota

Household category	Average change in real income			Poverty rate		Population
	Average	Poor	Nonpoor	Before	After	
	(percent change)			(percent)		(percent of total)
Viet Nam	1.5	1.7	1.4	25.0	24.7	100.0
Location						
Urban	-2.8	-5.4	-2.6	7.6	9.1	20.0
Rural	2.5	2.1	2.7	29.4	28.6	80.0
Region						
Northern Uplands	-0.7	-0.2	-0.9	34.9	36.1	16.7
Red River Delta	2.4	4.3	1.8	25.1	23.8	24.0
North Central Coast	0.4	1.2	-0.2	40.4	41.1	13.3
South Central Coast	-0.8	-0.3	-0.9	20.0	20.0	11.3
Central Highlands	-2.4	-2.2	-2.4	21.9	24.4	2.7
Southeast	-0.5	-0.6	-0.4	12.1	12.7	11.3
Mekong River Delta	5.6	4.0	5.9	17.2	15.4	20.7
Occupation						
Farmer	3.4	2.8	3.6	30.7	29.4	73.7
Nonfarmer	-3.9	-9.3	-3.4	9.1	11.8	26.3
Income group (quartile)						
Poorest	1.7	1.7	N.A.	100.0	91.6	25.0
2nd	1.1	N.A.	1.1	0.0	7.6	25.0
3rd	1.7	N.A.	1.7	0.0	0.0	25.0
Richest	1.4	N.A.	1.4	0.0	0.0	25.0

Source: Simulation using the Viet Nam Agricultural Spatial Equilibrium Model and household data from the Viet Nam Living Standards Survey (see text for details).

Note: Poverty is defined as households below the 25th percentile in terms of real per capita consumption expenditure. N.A. indicates not applicable (no household in that cell).

dominantly rural, so the nonpoor households are mostly commercial farmers rather than urban consumers.

Table 44 also shows the effect of eliminating the rice export quota on the poverty rate[34] for different types of households. The poverty rate rises in the urban areas (from 7.6 to 9.1 percent), while falling in the rural areas (from 29.4 to 28.6 percent). The overall poverty rate falls slightly from 25.0 to 24.7 percent. The poverty rate also de-

[34] The poverty rate is defined as the proportion of households falling below the poverty line, defined as the 25th percentile of per capita consumption expenditure in the original income distribution. Sensitivity analysis shows that using poverty lines at the 10th and 50th percentiles does not significantly affect the results.

clines among farmers and among households in the two surplus delta regions. The rate rises by more than 1 percentage point among nonfarmers and households in the Central Highlands and Northern Uplands.

Finally, Table 44 illustrates that there is some turnover in poor households as a result of the export liberalization. For 8.4 percent of the poor households, real income rises enough to lift them above the poverty line. At the same time, 7.6 percent of those in the second quartile fall below the poverty line. The net effect is a slight (0.3 percentage point) reduction in the proportion of households that are poor.

Alternative Rice Export Quota Levels

Complete export liberalization may not be politically acceptable given the negative impact on the urban poor described above. Thus, it is useful to examine the effect of partial liberalization. One approach would be to gradually raise the export quota. Table 45 shows the effect of raising the quota from 2.5 to 3.0, 3.5, 4.0, and 4.5 million tons. As the quota is relaxed, domestic rice prices and rice production increase, while rice consumption and world rice prices decline. Because the 4.5 million ton quota is not binding, the results are identical to the no-quota scenario shown in the last column.

Table 45 shows that the implicit export tax[35] falls from 22 percent with a 2.5 million ton quota to 9 percent with a 3.5 million ton quota, reaching 0 percent when the quota exceeds the free-market export level of 4.1 million tons. Similarly, the quota rent falls from US$151 million to zero over the same range. The net gains from liberalization (relative to the base scenario with the 2.5 million ton quota) rise as the quota is relaxed. It is notable that the incremental benefits diminish as one approaches complete liberalization. This is consistent with the general principle that the costs of trade distortions rise faster than the degree of distortion as measured by the implicit rate of tax or subsidy.

Replacing the Export Quota with an Export Tax

In a static setting, an export quota is equivalent to an export tax in terms of its effect on prices, production, and consumption.[36] Thus, replacing the export quota with an export tax would allow the government to limit exports and maintain low domestic prices, while generating tax revenue. It is true that the current quota system generates revenue for the government through contributions made by the state-owned enterprises (SOEs), including those that export rice. These contributions, however, are the result of negotiations rather than any specific formula, and government officials

---

[35] The implicit export tax is calculated as the shadow price on the quota constraint (the gap between domestic and world prices after adjustments for marketing and polishing) as a percentage of the with-quota world price.

[36] In a dynamic context, an export tax maintains a constant degree of (negative) protection over time, while allowing exports to vary. In contrast, an export quota maintains a constant level of exports, allowing the degree of protection to vary depending on domestic conditions and the world price.

Table 45—Effects of different rice export quotas

Variable/change	Base scenario: 2.5 millon ton quota	Partial relaxation of export quota (million ton quota) 3.0	3.5	4.0	4.5	No quota
Rice exports (million metric tons)	2.5	3.0	3.5	4.0	4.1	4.1
Implicit export tax (percent)	22.4	16.3	9.4	2.1	0.0	0.0
Quota rent (US$ million)	150.8	131.0	87.7	22.3	0.0	0.0
Change in household income (US$ million)	0.0	42.4	101.7	177.6	201.9	201.9
Change in total income (US$ million)	0.0	23.8	39.8	50.3	52.3	52.3
Percent change from base scenario						
Rice price	0.0	6.0	12.8	19.9	22.0	22.0
Paddy price	0.0	7.1	15.1	23.5	25.9	25.9
Rice production	0.0	2.3	4.9	7.4	8.1	8.1
Rice consumption	0.0	-1.3	-2.6	-3.9	-4.3	-4.3
Rice exports	0.0	18.5	38.2	58.0	63.5	63.5
Rice export price	0.0	-0.6	-1.3	-1.9	-2.1	-2.1
Rice export value	0.0	17.8	36.5	54.9	60.0	60.0
Household income	0.0	0.3	0.7	1.3	1.5	1.5
Total income	0.0	0.2	0.3	0.4	0.4	0.4

Source: Simulation using the Viet Nam Agricultural Spatial Equilibrium Model.

may not be aware of the full value of the quotas. An export tax would make the process more transparent and probably increase revenue.

Table 46 summarizes the effect of replacing the rice export quota with export taxes at different rates. An export tax of 25 percent represents a slight increase in export restrictions, compared with the base scenario, since the 1995 quota is equivalent to a 22 percent export tax. Thus, such a tax depresses prices, exports, production, and income slightly, while raising rice consumption. An export tax of 20 percent, in contrast, would represent a slight relaxation of export restrictions, having small effects in the opposite direction from those just described. Further reductions in the export tax would move prices, production, consumption, and exports gradually toward the free-trade levels.

As shown in the second section of Table 46, the tax revenue declines from US$157 million for a 25 percent tax to US$50 million for a 5 percent tax. Although not shown

Table 46—Effects of different rice export taxes

Variable/change	No quota and various export taxes 25 percent tax	20 percent tax	15 percent tax	10 percent tax	5 percent tax	No tax
Rice exports (million tons)	2.3	2.7	3.1	3.4	3.8	4.1
Tax revenue (US$ millions)	156.8	146.0	124.1	91.1	50.3	0.0
Change in household income (US$ million)	-15.1	15.7	53.0	96.4	146.1	201.9
Change in total income (US$ million)	-7.9	12.1	27.5	38.8	46.8	52.3
Percent change from base scenario						
Rice price	-2.6	2.4	7.3	12.3	17.1	22.0
Paddy price	-3.0	2.8	8.7	14.5	20.2	25.9
Rice production	-1.0	0.9	2.8	4.7	6.4	8.1
Rice consumption	0.6	-0.5	-1.5	-2.5	-3.4	-4.3
Rice exports	-8.2	7.5	22.4	36.7	50.3	63.5
Rice export price	0.3	-0.2	-0.7	-1.2	-1.7	-2.1
Rice export value	-7.9	7.2	21.5	35.0	47.8	60.0
Household income	-0.1	0.1	0.4	0.7	1.1	1.5
Total income	-0.1	0.1	0.2	0.3	0.3	0.4
Price index	-0.6	0.6	1.7	2.8	3.9	5.0

Source: Simulation using the Viet Nam Agricultural Spatial Equilibrium Model.

in the table, the model suggests that tax revenue also declines if the export tax is *raised* from 25 to 30 percent, because the reduction in exports more than offsets the increase in the tax rate. This suggests that, given domestic and international conditions of 1995, tax revenue would be maximized with a rate close to 25 percent. Total income, however, would be maximized by an export tax rate close to zero. The "optimal export tax" is close to zero because the export demand elasticity is high. As shown later, assuming a more inelastic world demand for Vietnamese rice would change this conclusion substantially.

Given the political constraints on export liberalization, one option would be to replace the export quota with an export tax and use part of the revenue to compensate those households hurt by the higher rice prices. The compensation could take the form of food-for-work or microcredit programs targeted at households and regions known to be negatively affected by the policy. According to the analysis presented here, rural nonfarming households, urban poor households, and rural households in the Central Highlands would merit special attention in such programs.

Sensitivity Analysis

Given the uncertainty regarding some of the parameters, it is useful to examine the sensitivity of the results to changes in the parameters. Table 47 shows the effect of removing the export quota under alternative supply and demand elasticities. The effect of quota removal on rice and paddy prices is not greatly affected by domestic supply and demand elasticities. This is because, in the absence of an export quota, Mekong rice prices are determined by the export price, and rice prices in the other regions are largely determined by transportation costs from the Mekong Delta region.

Rice prices are greatly affected, however, by the export demand elasticity. If export demand is relatively inelastic, then the increase in exports depresses world prices and thus dampens the increase in domestic prices. Similarly, an elasticity of –1,000 (close to the perfect elasticity of the small-country assumption) would result in domestic prices rising virtually all the way to the original world price.

When the quota is removed, production and exports are naturally higher (lower) with a more (less) elastic supply than in the original simulation. Rice exports are just 3.3 million tons if the price elasticity of rice supply is 0.1, but 4.9 million tons if the elasticity is 0.6. Similarly, a more (less) elastic demand for rice means that consumption falls more (less) with the elimination of the export quota. Exports are 3.8 million tons with a more inelastic demand (–0.1), compared with 4.7 million tons with a more elastic demand (–0.6). In all scenarios, however, the quota removal results in relatively large increases in exports (32 to 93 percent).

The gains to Vietnamese households from export liberalization range from US$149 to US$230 million within the range of parameter assumptions shown in Table 47. The gains in total income (including the exporters= loss in quota rents) vary between –US$1 million and US$80 million. The gains from liberalization appear to be most sensitive to the export demand elasticity, at least given the range tested here. If the export demand elasticity is relatively inelastic (–8), Viet Nam actually loses slightly as a result of removing the rice export quota, though households still gain due to the transfer from export SOEs. This is because the terms-of-trade losses related to the lower world rice price (area *E* in Figure 8) is greater than the reduction in deadweight loss (areas *B* + *D*). If the export demand elasticity is high (–1,000), implying that Vietnamese exports have virtually no effect on world prices, the gains from liberalization are US$230 million for households and US$80 million for the nation as a whole.

The income elasticity of rice has very little effect on the results because the percentage change in income is relatively small, much smaller than the percentage change in prices, for example. Furthermore, the income elasticity for rice and the other staples is modest. Thus, the feedback from food market to income back to food markets is not large.

Given the sensitivity of the results to assumptions about the export demand elasticity for Vietnamese rice, this issue is explored in more detail. Figure 9 shows the benefits in total income and household income from different levels of export quota and different assumptions regarding the export demand elasticity for Vietnamese rice

Table 47—Sensitivity analysis of the effect of eliminating the rice export quota

Variable/change	Original assumptions	Price elasticity of rice supply		Price elasticity of local rice demand		Income elasticity of rice demand		Price elasticity of world rice demand	
		0.1	0.6	-0.1	-0.6	0.0	0.8	-8	-1,000
Rice exports (million tons)	4.1	3.3	4.9	3.8	4.7	4.1	4.0	3.8	4.3
Change in household income (US$ million)	201.9	216.1	188.9	208.1	193.1	201.9	203.5	148.7	229.6
Change in total income (US$ million)	52.3	66.5	39.3	58.5	43.5	52.3	53.9	-0.9	80.0
Percent change from base scenario: 2.5 million ton export quota									
Rice price	22.0	23.1	20.9	22.3	21.0	22.0	21.9	17.4	24.2
Paddy price	25.9	27.3	24.5	26.5	24.9	25.9	26.1	20.5	28.6
Rice production	8.1	2.1	13.7	8.3	7.8	8.1	8.1	6.5	8.8
Rice consumption	-4.3	-4.5	-4.1	-1.0	-9.2	-4.3	-3.4	-3.4	-4.7
Rice exports	63.5	31.7	93.4	49.6	83.8	63.5	59.9	51.0	69.3
Rice export price	-2.1	-1.1	-3.1	-1.7	-2.8	-2.1	-2.0	-6.4	-0.1
Rice export value	60.0	30.4	87.4	47.1	78.7	60.0	56.7	41.4	69.2
Household income	1.5	1.6	1.4	1.5	1.4	1.5	1.5	1.1	1.7
Total income	0.4	0.5	0.3	0.4	0.3	0.4	0.4	-0.0	0.6
Price index	5.0	5.2	4.8	5.1	4.8	5.0	5.0	4.0	5.5

Source: Simulation using the Viet Nam Agricultural Spatial Equilibrium Model.

(*e*). Household benefits (the dark lines) rise sharply as the quota is relaxed and are not initially affected by the export demand elasticity. This is because, as long as the quota is binding, the size of the quota (and not international prices) determine domestic prices and hence household income. Once the quota becomes nonbinding, further increases in the quota have no effect on prices or household income, so the line in Figure 9 becomes horizontal. The more inelastic the world demand for Vietnamese rice, the lower the free-trade level of rice exports and the sooner that the quota becomes nonbinding.

In contrast, the effect of quota relaxation on total income (the gray lines) varies depending on the export demand elasticity. Total income is the sum of household income and the quota rents received by rice exporters. A more inelastic world demand for Vietnamese rice implies that quota relaxation has a larger negative effect on world prices, thus causing more rapid reduction in quota rents. When the quota becomes nonbinding, the quota rent disappears and further increases in the quota have no effect.

With an inelastic world demand (–8), there are small losses because the loss of the quota rents slightly exceeds the gains to households. In this case, a quota of 3.0 million tons is similar to an "optimal" export tax, which takes advantage of Viet Nam's market power to raise world prices slightly. In the base scenario, with an elasticity of –12, the gains in total income from quota relaxation reach US$52 million per year when the quota becomes nonbinding (at 4.2 million tons). Similarly, with an elasticity of –1,000, the gains reach US$80 million when the quota becomes nonbinding (at 4.3 million tons).

These results highlight the importance of the elasticity of world demand for Vietnamese rice exports to Viet Nam. One implication is that further research on the magnitude of this elasticity would assist the formulation of rice export policy. Another implication is that Viet Nam has a strong interest in lobbying for liberalization of world rice markets in international fora such as the World Trade Organization and ASEAN. Trade liberalization among rice importers would increase elasticity of world demand for Vietnamese rice and thus increase the benefits of export liberalization in Viet Nam.

Liberalization of Internal Marketing

In 1995–96 when the IFPRI survey was carried out, there were various restrictions on the movement of food, particularly rice, from one region to another. These restrictions took the form of fees, taxes, police checkpoints, requirements for permits, and occasionally outright bans (see Chapter 3). In some cases, the restrictions were implemented by government authorities and in other cases by local officials acting on their own. The effect of these restrictions was to raise the cost of moving goods from one region to another, thus creating a price difference between the two regions that exceeded the cost of transportation.

In the base scenario, the price differential between two regions is not allowed to exceed either the cost of transportation (based on the IFPRI trader survey) or the observed price differential (based on government price data), whichever is greater.

Figure 9—Benefits of relaxing the rice export quota with alternative export demand elasticities

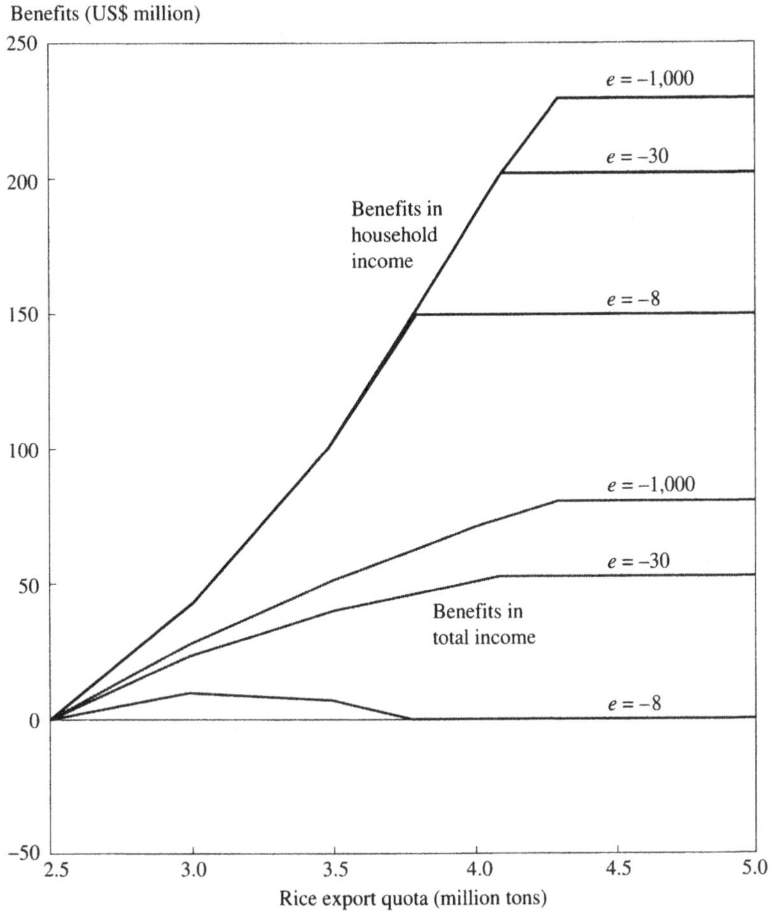

Source: Simulations using the Viet Nam Agricultural Spatial Equilibrium Model.

When the observed price differential is greater than the cost of transportation, the difference is likely to be related to restrictions on internal trade. The removal of these restrictions is simulated by redefining the maximum price differential as the cost of transportation.

Table 48 compares the national results of the base scenario (with restrictions on internal trade) and the simulation with no internal restrictions but maintaining the export quota. Average rice and paddy prices fall slightly, as does rice production and consumption. In spite of these modest effects, total income rises US$45.6 million (0.3 percent), almost as much as the long-term export liberalization scenario that involved much larger average price changes. The explanation is that the national average hides strong regional patterns.

As shown in Table 49, rice prices fall in the north and rise in the south as a result

Table 48—Overall effects of removing restrictions on internal trade

Variable	Unit	Base scenario (restriction on internal trade)	Removing restrictions on internal trade	Percent change
Rice price	Dong/kilogram	2,781	2,681	-3.6
Paddy price	Dong/kilogram	1,503	1,482	-1.4
Paddy production	1,000 tons	24,949	24,845	-0.4
Rice production	1,000 tons	13,865	13,807	-0.4
Rice consumption	1,000 tons	11,333	11,275	-0.5
Rice exports	1,000 tons	2,532	2,532	0.0
Rice export price	US$/ton	269	269	0.0
Rice export value	US$ million	681	681	0.0
Household income	US$ million/year	13,567	13,645	0.6
Total income	US$ million/year	13,716	13,762	0.3
Price index	base = 100	100	98	-1.2

Source: Simulation using the Viet Nam Agricultural Spatial Equilibrium Model.

of reduced south-north transportation costs. These price changes cause production to fall in the north and rise in the south, while consumption moves in the opposite direction in each region. Thus, the Mekong rice surplus rises from 4.49 to 4.65 million tons. Since exports are held constant by the quota, all of the additional 160,000 tons of Mekong surplus are being shipped to deficit regions within Viet Nam. At the same time, the lower prices in the north imply that the Red River Delta surpluses are much smaller (57,000 tons, down from 154,000 tons), leaving the region barely covering its own requirements.

One interesting result is that internal liberalization reduces the value of the rice export quotas. The implicit tax associated with the quota falls from US$60 per ton (22 percent of the world price) to US$49 per ton (18 percent). Since internal market liberalization gives the Mekong Delta better access to rice markets in northern Viet Nam, the export quota is less binding.

The convergence of north and south rice prices has some distributional effects as well. Surplus rice farmers can be expected to gain in the south and lose in the north, while urban and deficit rural households gain in the north but lose in the south. These expectations are borne out in Table 50. The Northern Uplands, being a northern deficit region, gains, as does the Mekong River Delta, being a southern surplus region. The Red River Delta loses, because its surplus farmers are hurt by the lower rice prices. Urban households gain, particularly the poor. The effect on all rural households is neutral, though the rural poor lose. Generally, the effects are small, with

Table 49—Regional effects of removing restrictions on internal trade

Region	Rice price	Rice production	Rice consumption	Rice surplus
	(dong/kilogram)		(1,000 metric tons)	
Levels with no restriction simulation				
Northern Uplands	2,840	1,175	2,003	-828
Red River Delta	2,699	2,501	2,444	57
North Central Coast	2,848	1,172	1,515	-343
South Central Coast	2,807	984	1,116	-131
Central Highlands	2,677	242	491	-249
Southeast	2,513	524	1,152	-628
Mekong River Delta	2,466	7,209	2,555	4,654
Change from base scenario (with restrictions)				
		(percent)		
Northern Uplands	-11.8	-5.1	0.9	11.0
Red River Delta	-9.4	-3.7	0.0	-63.0
North Central Coast	-6.1	-2.6	0.2	11.4
South Central Coast	3.6	1.2	-1.4	-16.9
Central Highlands	0.8	-0.1	-0.3	-0.8
Southeast	5.0	1.2	-1.6	-3.7
Mekong River Delta	5.2	1.6	-1.7	3.6

Source: Simulation using the Viet Nam Agricultural Spatial Equilibrium Model.

most being less than 1 percentage point. The poverty rate falls in urban areas but remains unchanged among rural households. Poverty falls slightly in the three northern deficit regions and in the southern surplus region (Mekong), while rising in the two southern deficit regions and the northern surplus region. On a national level, these effects tend to cancel each other out, leaving the overall poverty rate unaffected by internal market liberalization.

What is the effect of removing restrictions on the internal movement of food *and* removing the rice export quota? Table 51 reveals that internal market liberalization would dampen the increase in prices associated with export liberalization. Rice prices rise 22 percent as a result of quota removal alone (see Table 42), but just 14 percent when quota removal is combined with internal market liberalization. Mekong prices are virtually the same in the two scenarios, being set by world prices. Thus, the entire reduction in south-north transportation costs is passed on to northern rice markets in the form of lower prices. Rice exports are 3.8 million tons, substantially above the quota level of 2.5 million tons but slightly below the level achieved by

Table 50—Distributional effects of removing restrictions on internal trade

Household category	Average change in real income			Poverty rate		Population
	Average	Poor	Nonpoor	Before	After	
	(percent change)			(percent)		(percent of total)
Viet Nam	0.1	-0.2	0.2	25.0	25.0	100.0
Location						
Urban	0.4	0.8	0.4	7.6	7.5	20.0
Rural	0.0	-0.3	0.1	29.4	29.4	80.0
Region						
Northern Uplands	0.7	0.5	0.8	34.9	34.7	16.7
Red River Delta	-0.8	-1.5	-0.6	25.1	26.0	24.0
North Central Coast	0.0	-0.2	0.2	40.4	40.1	13.3
South Central Coast	-0.2	-0.1	-0.2	20.0	19.9	11.3
Central Highlands	-0.1	-0.1	-0.1	21.9	22.7	2.7
Southeast	-0.1	-0.2	-0.1	12.1	12.5	11.3
Mekong River Delta	1.0	0.6	1.1	17.2	16.4	20.7
Occupation						
Farmer	0.1	-0.2	0.2	30.7	30.6	73.7
Nonfarmer	0.0	-0.6	0.1	9.1	9.3	26.3
Income group (quartile)						
Poorest	-0.2	-0.2	N.A.	100.0	97.6	25.0
2nd	-0.0	N.A.	-0.0	0.0	2.5	25.0
3rd	0.2	N.A.	0.2	0.0	0.0	25.0
Richest	0.4	N.A.	0.4	0.0	0.0	25.0

Source: Simulation using the Viet Nam Agricultural Spatial Equilibrium Model and household data from the Viet Nam Living Standards Survey (see text for details).

Note: Poverty is defined as households below the 25th percentile in terms of real per capita consumption expenditure.

quota removal alone (compare Tables 42 and 51). The reason is that internal market liberalization facilitates shipments of Mekong surpluses to deficit regions within the country, thus competing somewhat with exports.

Combining quota removal and internal liberalization raises household income US$232 million and total income US$83 million. These figures are larger than either reform individually, but less than the sum of the benefits. In other words, there are no complementarities in combining internal and export liberalization, at least within this static partial-equilibrium model. As noted above, internal market liberalization provides an alternative outlet for Mekong rice surpluses, thus reducing the implicit tax associated with the quota. As a result, the additional benefits of quota removal are smaller than when starting from the base scenario with internal restrictions.

Table 51—Overall effects of eliminating the rice export quota and removing restrictions on internal trade

Variable	Unit	Base scenario (restriction on internal trade)	Eliminate quota and remove internal restrictions	Percent change
Rice price	Dong/kilogram	2,781.2	3,176.4	14.2
Paddy price	Dong/kilogram	1,503.0	1,801.7	19.9
Paddy production	1,000 tons	24,949.2	26,508.3	6.2
Rice production	1,000 tons	13,865.5	14,732.0	6.2
Rice consumption	1,000 tons	11,333.5	10,893.0	-3.9
Rice exports	1,000 tons	2,532.0	3,839.0	51.6
Rice export price	US$/ton	269.0	264.4	-1.7
Rice export value	US$ million	681.1	1,014.9	49.0
Household income	US$ million/year	13,567.2	13,799.5	1.7
Total income	US$ million/year	13,716.8	13,799.5	0.6
Price index	base = 100	100.0	102.8	2.8

Source: Simulation using the Viet Nam Agricultural Spatial Equilibrium Model.

The lack of complementarity between internal and export liberalization probably reflects the specific geographic patterns of Vietnamese rice marketing rather than any universal tendency. For example, if rice had to be transported overland from the surplus region to the port, internal market liberalization would facilitate exports rather than creating an alternative market. In this context, internal market liberalization would make an export quota more binding, so that combining the two reforms would generate benefits greater than the sum of the gains from the two reforms implemented separately.

Epilogue

The results of this analysis were presented in various seminars and workshops in late 1996. Since that time, the government has implemented some of the liberalization measures discussed here, allowing us to make a preliminary assessment of the actual impact of the reforms.

In March 1997, the government issued Decree No. 140/TTg, which raised the rice export quota to 3.5 million tons and decentralized much of the quota allocation process to provincial authorities. In addition, the decree set quotas for the whole year rather than for a part of the year, as had been done in the past.

The quota was raised to 4.0 million tons in 1998, and four criteria were established for private-sector participation in rice exports (Decision 12/TTg of January 1998).

Table 52—Comparison of domestic and export prices since 1995

Year	Retail rice price Mekong Delta	Exchange rate	Retail rice price Mekong Delta	Viet Nam f.o.b. 25 percent broken rice price	Thailand f.o.b. 25 percent broken rice price	Ratio of Mekong price to 25% f.o.b. VN price	Ratio of Mekong price to 25% f.o.b. Thai price
	(dong/ kilogram)	(dong/US$)		(US$/metric tons)			(ratio)
1995	2,760	11,043	250	252	300	0.99	0.83
1996	2,790	11,038	253	250	280	1.01	0.90
1997	2,707	11,905	227	229	254	0.99	0.90
1998	3,411	13,483	253	250	250	1.01	1.01
1999	3,162	13,963	226	205	215	1.10	1.05

Source: Compiled by the Ministry of Agriculture and Rural Development (MARD), Viet Nam, from Government Price Committee data.

Later that year, export permits were temporarily suspended in response to a below-average harvest in the north, but exports reached the quota limit in any case.

In 1999, the quota was increased to 4.5 million tons, and, for the first time, private traders were allocated quotas, albeit just 4 percent of the total. Some observers believe that the rice export quota is no longer binding, that Viet Nam could not export more than 4.5 million tons even without a quota (Ross Kreamer, personal communication).

Table 52 shows the trends in rice prices during the period 1995–99, when the exports rose from 2.5 to 4.5 million tons. The retail price of rice in the Mekong Delta has been stable or declined in dollar terms since 1995, contrary to the expected effect of export liberalization. It should be recalled, however, that the model simulates the effect of export liberalization on domestic prices, holding other factors equal, but other factors have not remained equal: in particular, international prices have fallen.

A better measure of the impact of rice policy is to look at the margin between Mekong prices and international prices. For international prices, the Vietnamese and Thai export prices (f.o.b.) for 25 percent broken rice are used. As shown in the last two columns of Table 52, Mekong prices have increased from 99 to 110 percent of the Vietnamese f.o.b. price, and from 83 to 105 percent of Thai f.o.b. prices (presumably, they exceed world prices because of domestic marketing margins).

Decree No. 140/TTg of March 1997 also lifted restrictions on internal rice trade and eliminated some licenses and controls on transport. Data are not available on the volumes of rice transported from south to north, but price data suggest that the decree had the expected effect of increasing north-south trade. As shown in Table 53, retail prices in the Northern Uplands have fallen from 22 percent above Mekong

Table 53—Comparison of Mekong and Red River Delta rice since 1995

Year	Nominal retail rice price			Ratio of Northern Uplands to Mekong price	Ratio of Red River Delta to Mekong price
	Northern Uplands	Red River Delta	Mekong River Delta		
	(dong/kilogram)			(ratio)	
1995	3,380	3,300	2,760	1.22	1.20
1996	3,470	3,400	2,790	1.24	1.22
1997	2,849	2,707	2,707	1.05	1.00
1998	3,595	3,448	3,411	1.05	1.01
1999	3,571	3,343	3,162	1.13	1.06

Source: Compiled by the Ministry of Agriculture and Rural Development (MARD), Viet Nam, from Government Price Committee data.

prices to 13 percent above, while prices in the Red River Delta have declined from 20 percent above to 6 percent above. In both cases, the largest drop was between 1996 (before the decree) to 1997 (the year of the decree).

Conclusions

VASEM is useful for examining the impact of alternative rice marketing policies. With regard to the rice export quota, the model indicates that there is some justification for the concern of the Vietnamese government that eliminating rice export quotas would raise prices and hurt some Vietnamese households. The model confirms that rice prices would rise 14 to 22 percent (depending on whether internal restrictions were also removed) and have an adverse effect on urban households, nonfarm rural households, and households in the Central Highlands. At the same time, the model shows that the net gains to rice farmers and consumers would be around US$200 million. Three-quarters of this would represent a transfer from SOEs exporting rice and one-quarter a net gain to the country. Furthermore, poor households tend to gain both in absolute terms and relative to nonpoor households because they are predominantly rural farmers who benefit from higher rice prices.

In order to phase in the effects over time, the government could liberalize rice exports slowly by replacing the quota with an export tax and gradually reducing the tax rate. The model indicates that a 22 percent tax would be equivalent to the 2.5 million tons quota. This option has the advantage of generating revenue that could be used to alleviate the impact of higher rice prices through targeted assistance.

With regard to restrictions on internal movement of food, the model suggests that the impact on *average* prices and incomes would be relatively small. Nonetheless, the absolute gains are large compared to the negligible costs of such a policy. Removing restrictions on internal trade would have substantial regional effects, however, lowering prices in the north and raising them in the south. The distributional effects are relatively small and tend to cancel each other, so there is virtually no change in the national poverty rate.

Since 1996 when the results of this analysis were presented, the export quota has been relaxed significantly and the restrictions on the internal movement of rice abolished. Preliminary evidence for the period 1995–99 suggest that, as expected, the margin between the Mekong Delta price and export prices has narrowed, as have the margins between rice prices in the north and south of Viet Nam.

CHAPTER 7

Conclusions and Policy Implications

The historical record is fairly clear that market liberalization has had a positive effect on economic growth, agricultural production, and the rice sector. Rice production responded briefly to the adoption of the contract system in 1980 and more vigorously to the decollectivization and liberalization of trade, implemented in 1988–90. Since that time, rice production has grown at an annual rate of more than 5 percent. In 1989 Viet Nam began exporting rice and became the third largest exporter. Contrary to the predictions of some analysts, rice exports were not only sustained, they increased, making Viet Nam the second largest rice exporter in 1997.

What has been the effect on poverty? It is argued frequently that even if market liberalization enhances growth and reduces poverty in the long run, the poor bear the burden of adjustment in the short run. Although there are no estimates of changes in Vietnamese poverty rates over time, indirect evidence suggests that this is not the case in Viet Nam. Survey data reveal that 93 to 95 percent of the poor live in rural areas, and rural incomes appear to have risen with the reforms. First, agricultural production, rice production, and apparent rice consumption per capita have risen significantly since the mid-1980s. Second, the community survey of the 1992–93 VLSS found that 95 percent of the communes reported an improvement in living standards over the previous five years. Of these communes, 94 percent identified agricultural policies as the main reason for the improvement. Third, there is a consensus that ownership of consumer durables such as televisions and motorbikes has increased rapidly even in rural areas.

In spite of these gains, poverty rates are still high, and the benefits of liberalization have probably not been distributed equally among regions and between urban and rural areas. Policymakers are concerned about the distributional implications of further liberalization of the rice markets, a concern that is manifested in binding rice export quotas.

Policy Implications

This study uses a spatial equilibrium multimarket model to simulate the impact of alternative rice marketing policies, focusing in particular on the effects of further market liberalization. The results indicate that export liberalization would raise the price of rice and hurt the urban poor and rice-deficit households. At the same time, the gains to the rural sector, particularly farmers in the delta regions, outweigh these effects, resulting in a slight reduction in overall poverty and an increase in household and national income.

The model also shows that converting the export quota into an export tax would be one approach to achieving the distributional goals of the quota, while improving transparency and generating government revenue for targeted antipoverty programs.

The model also highlights the fact that the gains from rice export liberalization depend heavily on the elasticity of demand for Vietnamese rice exports on world markets. The more elastic is world rice demand, the larger the benefits to Viet Nam of export liberalization. This implies that the government could use more accurate estimates of the export demand elasticity for rice in its policymaking process. In addition, it suggests that Viet Nam has a strong interest in using international fora to lobby for trade liberalization in rice markets, particularly among importing countries.

Somewhat surprisingly, the aggregate effects on income and poverty of removing restrictions on internal trade are of the same order of importance as the liberalization of external trade. Internal liberalization slightly benefits the poor in urban areas and deficit areas in the north, while it slightly penalizes the poor in rural areas.

The combination of internal and external liberalization does not necessarily result in complementarity of effects. Even though overall income grows by more than it does in each policy separately, it grows by less than the sum. This is more a reflection of the structure of transportation and commodity flows in Viet Nam than a general point about the complementarity of policies.

More generally, it is clear that future growth in the rice sector depends on exports, and export expansion depends on the development of an effective marketing system able to meet the changing needs of domestic and international markets at low cost. The development of such a system relies heavily on the participation of the private sector. The private sector has responded to reforms, but it is still constrained by the SOE monopoly on exports and limited access to credit and information. Domestic markets are only weakly integrated as a result of an underdeveloped infrastructure system, policy restrictions on interregional movements, and lack of transparency and credibility of policy announcement.

The government of Viet Nam is taking steps to address these problems. In March 1997, restrictions on the internal movement of rice were abolished. In addition, the export quota was relaxed, reaching 4.5 million tons in 1999. Finally, the government is currently issuing export permits to some private millers in the Mekong Delta. Although these are positive steps, successful market reform requires not only removing policy restrictions on trade but strengthening the role of the government in providing market information and infrastructure, supporting research and extension, developing the legal and financial infrastructure needed to promote efficient, competitive markets.

Lessons for Other Countries

What lessons can the Vietnamese experience with market reform offer to other countries? The first lesson is that relatively equal distribution of land assets is a key ingredient for the poverty-reducing effect of market reform. While in other Asian countries the proportion of landless is around 20 percent of the population in rural areas, in Viet Nam the landless population is barely 2 percent. Most farmers are smallholders, and even the poor have land assets that allow them to cultivate rice. Thus, an increase in the rice price would generally imply an increase in income for the majority of farmers. A similar policy in a country where a small percentage of the population owns a large amount of land would probably have an adverse effect on poverty.

Second, the potential offered by market reform cannot be translated into actual growth unless other material and institutional conditions are in place. In the case of rice in Viet Nam, most notable among these other conditions was a relatively good irrigation and extension system. The government of Viet Nam invested heavily in irrigation infrastructure construction and rehabilitation even before market reforms were adopted. Its extension service was also relatively successful in disseminating modern technology such as high-yielding varieties, fertilizers, and plant protection techniques. The success of the technology dissemination was helped by the existence of a relatively well-educated labor force, with literacy rates much higher than in the majority of countries at a similar level of development. Good rice seeds, adequate irrigation, and knowledge of modern agronomic techniques were largely present when market reforms were initiated. The strong response of the private sector to market incentives followed.

Third, an export-oriented strategy can be consistent with food security and with smallholder production. Policymakers' fear that liberalizing rice exports would create widespread food insecurity and exacerbate poverty is understandable, but this analysis demonstrates that it is largely unfounded. Although export liberalization does create winners and losers, the net effect on poverty is negligible or slightly positive.

Fourth, the regional and distributional dimensions need to be taken into consideration in the analysis of policy reform. Since some groups will gain and others will lose from policy reforms, nationally beneficial policies may be blocked by regions or groups that expect to lose. Analysis in which the impact can be broken down by region and by group helps identify and quantify these trade-offs, rather than ignoring them. In fact, a better understanding of the trade-offs may be useful in designing policies (such as transfers and taxes) that at least partially offset the distributional bias of policy reform. A spatial equilibrium model is useful in providing a regionally disaggregated analysis of the impact of policy. In particular, the model highlighted the fact that the impact of trade liberalization is dampened as one moves away from the trading region of the country. Finally, this study demonstrates how a spatial equilibrium model can be combined with household marketing data to provide rich detail on the distributional impact of policy options within and across regions.

APPENDIX 1

Methods to Analyze Market Integration

The simplest way to measure market integration is to consider correlation of price series at different markets. This is intuitively related to the idea that integrated markets exhibit prices that move together. Price correlations are the easiest way to measure these co-movements. However, the traditional tests of market integration focused on correlation coefficients of spatial prices ignore the presence of other factors, such as general price inflation, seasonality, population growth, and procurement policy (see Lele 1972 for India, Farruk 1970 for Bangladesh, Jones 1972 for Nigeria).

A second approach is to consider correlation of price differences (see Blyn 1973, Harriss 1979, and Timmer 1974). This approach has the attractive property of interpreting market integration as the interdependence of price changes in different markets. Moreover, price changes would largely eliminate common trends that introduce spurious correlation.

A third approach is to study the cointegration of price series. Prices move from time to time, and their margins are subject to various shocks. When a long-run linear relation exists among different price series, these series are said to be cointegrated (Engle and Granger 1987). The presence of cointegration between two series is indicative of strong interdependence; its absence indicates market segmentation. Often, it is not enough to say that markets are integrated. One would like to know the extent of integration. Segmentation occurs when there is no cointegration. *Perfect integration* occurs if the price in one market is just a translation of the price in the other market, implying that price changes are the same. The translation factor can be interpreted as a transfer cost between the two markets. Segmentation occurs when there is no relationship between prices in different markets. However, it is only in extreme cases that perfect integration or segmentation occurs. Most of the time, intermediate degrees of integration occur. Analytically, the major effort is to make precise the measurement of these different degrees of integration. This is achieved by measuring the *magnitude* of price transmission with the help of *dynamic multipliers* (λ_{ij}). The analysis of dynamic adjustments also allows us to compute the *speed* of price transmission.

Method of Calculating Dynamic Multipliers

The immediate impact of price shocks should be distinguished from the impact that is building over time. The process of price transmission usually takes time, owing to the complex dynamic adjustments. Following Ravallion (1986), one can then distinguish between the short and the long runs and dynamic multipliers computed from estimation of equations such as

$$p_{i,t} = \sum_{k=1}^{k=m_i} \alpha_{i,k}\, p_{i,t-k} + \sum_{h=0}^{h=n_i} \beta_{i,h}\, p_{j,t-h} + X_{i,t}\, \gamma_i + \varepsilon_{i,t}, \tag{7}$$

where $p_{i,t}$ is the price of rice in market i at time t, $p_{j,t}$ is the price of rice in market j at time t; X_{it} are exogenous variables such as seasonal dummies and time trend, and $\varepsilon_{i,t}$ is an error term. $\alpha_{i,k}$, $\beta_{i,h}$, and γ_i are coefficients to be estimated, and m_i, and n_j are the number of lags of prices in market i and j, respectively.

In the estimation, problems of simultaneity may be encountered, related to the contemporaneous use of price in market i and market j. Since both prices may respond to the same type of shocks, the error term $\varepsilon_{i,t}$ is expected to be correlated with the price $p_{j,t}$. To overcome this problem, an instrumental variables estimation of $p_{j,t}$ has been used, taking lagged values of the prices of all markets included in the study. The three lags, one for prices in market i, one for prices in market j, and one for the instrumental variables, are determined simultaneously by application of the Akaike information criterion (Akaike 1969).

The *magnitude of price adjustment* is estimated with dynamic multipliers. Dynamic multipliers are interpreted as the effect of a price change due to a random shock or a shift in an exogenous variable. In the context of the model introduced above, the cumulative effect of a shock to the price in market j on the price in market i, after k periods is denoted by $\lambda^{i,j}_k$

$$\lambda^{ij}_k = \sum_{h=0}^{k} \frac{\partial E_t p}{\partial p_j}, \tag{8}$$

where E_t denotes the expectation operator based on information available at time t. The full adjustment of the dynamic process described by the model is given by the long-run dynamic multiplier, which corresponds to

$$\lambda^{ij}_{\infty} = \lim_{k \to \infty} \lambda^{ij}_k. \tag{9}$$

Method of Calculating the Speed of Adjustment

The definition of the long term multiplier $\lambda^{i,j}{}_4$ allows one to define the speed of convergence $\tau^{i,j}{}_4$ as the first time after which the percentage deviations of the interim multiplier from the long-term multiplier are "small enough." That is, for a given tolerance limit $\in$, for every $k > \tau^{i,j}{}_{4,}$ one has

$$\left| \frac{\lambda^{ij}_{k} - \lambda^{ij}_{\infty}}{\lambda^{ij}_{\infty}} \right| . \qquad (10)$$

In the computations, the tolerance limit has been taken equal to 1 percent.

Sometimes, the speed of the response of prices is related to the efficiency of the market system. However, this assumption is not always valid. Rapid adjustments are just an indication of the flexibility of the mechanism. They do not necessarily imply well functioning systems. Within the context of this discussion, it is important to consider the speed of adjustment as just one dimension of integration. Given two markets, A and B, with the same value of the magnitude of price adjustment with respect to a third market C, then the shorter the time to complete this adjustment, the better integrated the market.

APPENDIX 2

Derivation of Welfare Measures

The impact of a price change on household welfare can be decomposed into the impact on the household as a consumer of the good and the impact on the household as a producer of the good. These two effects are considered in order.

Effect of Price Changes on Households as Consumers

The impact of price changes on consumers is often calculated using consumer surplus. A similar but more theoretically consistent concept is compensating variation, defined as the amount of money needed to compensate a consumer for the price change and restore the original utility level. The compensating variation change can be written as the difference between two values of the expenditure function:

$$CV = e(\mathbf{p}_1, u_0) - e(\mathbf{p}_0, u_0), \tag{11}$$

where CV is the compensating variation, $e(.)$ is the expenditure function, $\mathbf{p}$ is a vector of prices, u is utility, and the subscripts refer to before (0) and after (1) the price change. This can be approximated using a second-order Taylor-series expansion:

$$CV \cong \frac{1}{1!} \sum_{i=1}^{n} \frac{\partial e(\mathbf{p}_0, u_0)}{\partial p_i} (p_{1i} - p_{0i}) + \frac{1}{2!} \sum_{i=1}^{n} \sum_{j=1}^{n} \frac{\partial^2 e(\mathbf{p}_0, u_0)}{\partial p_i \partial p_i} (p_{1i} - p_{0i}) \; (p_{1j} - p_{0j}). \tag{12}$$

Using Shephard's lemma and replacing $(p_{1i} - p_{0i})$ by Δp_i yields

$$CV \cong \sum_{i=1}^{n} h_i(\mathbf{p}_0, u_0) \; \Delta p_i + \frac{1}{2} \sum_{i=1}^{n} \sum_{j=1}^{n} \frac{\partial h_i(\mathbf{p}_0, u_0)}{\partial p_j} \Delta p_i \, \Delta p_j \tag{13}$$

where $h_i(\mathbf{p}_0, u_0)$ is the Hicksian demand for the good i given the original price vector $\mathbf{p}_0$. If the Hicksian demand is replaced with $qi(\mathbf{p}_0, x_0)$, the Marshallian demand at the original income level, the expression is the same as that used in the calculation of real income within the Viet Nam Agricultural Spatial Equilibrium Model (VASEM) (see equation 4 in Appendix 4).

A slightly different form of the same equation is used to calculate the household-level welfare impact of rice price changes. To simplify, the calculations are limited to the impact of changes in the rice price on purchasing power. The partial in the second term is converted into the Hicksian own-price elasticity of demand, replacing the Hicksian demand, $h(\mathbf{p_0}, u_0)$, with the Marshallian demand at the original income level, $q(\mathbf{p_0}, x_0)$, where x_0 is the original income, giving the following:

$$CV \cong q_r(\mathbf{p_0}, x_0)\, \Delta p_r + \frac{1}{2}\, \varepsilon_{rr}^{H} \frac{q_r(\mathbf{p_0}, x_0)}{p_{0r}}\, \Delta p_r\, \Delta p_r, \tag{14}$$

where q_r and p_r are the quantity demanded and the price of rice, respectively, and $\in_{rr}^{H}$ is the own-price Hicksian demand elasticity of rice. After dividing both sides by the original income (x_0) and multiplying the top and bottom of the right side by P_{0r}, the result is

$$\frac{CV}{x_0} \cong \frac{p_{0r}\, q_r(\mathbf{p_0}, x_0)}{x_0} \frac{\Delta p_r}{p_{0r}} + \frac{1}{2}\, \varepsilon_{rr}^{H} \frac{p_{0r}\, q_r(\mathbf{p_0}, u_0)}{p_{0r} x_0} \left| \frac{\Delta p_r}{p_{0r}} \right|^2. \tag{15}$$

Finally, CR_r, the consumption ratio for rice, which is defined as the value of rice consumption as a proportion of income (or total expenditure), is substituted:

$$\frac{CV}{x_0} \cong CR_r \frac{\Delta p_r}{p_{0r}} + \frac{1}{2}\, \varepsilon_{rr}^{H}\, CR_r \left| \frac{\Delta p_r}{p_{0r}} \right|^2. \tag{16}$$

Effect of Price Changes on Households as Producers

Turning to the effect of a price change on the household as producer, the algebra is similar to that described above except that one starts with the profit function. The change in income can be written as follows:

$$\Delta x = \pi(\mathbf{p_1}, \mathbf{w_0}, \mathbf{z_0}) - \pi(\mathbf{p_0}, \mathbf{w_0}, \mathbf{z_0}), \tag{17}$$

where Δx is the change in income, $\pi(.)$ is the profit function, $\mathbf{p}$ is a vector of output prices, $\mathbf{w}$ is a vector of input prices, $\mathbf{z}$ is a vector of fixed factor quantities, and the subscripts refer to before (0) and after (1) the price change. This can be approximated using a second-order Taylor-series expansion:

$$\Delta x \cong \frac{1}{1!} \sum_{i=1}^{n} \frac{\partial \pi(\mathbf{p_0}, \mathbf{w_0}, \mathbf{z_0})}{\partial p_i} (p_{1i} - p_{0i}) + \frac{1}{2!} \sum_{i=1}^{n} \sum_{j=1}^{n} \frac{\partial \pi^2(\mathbf{p_0}, \mathbf{w_0}, \mathbf{z_0})}{\partial p_i \partial p_j} (p_{1i} - p_{0i})(p_{1j} - p_{0j}). \tag{18}$$

Using Shephard's lemma and replacing $(p_{1i} - p_{0i})$ by Δp_i gives

$$x \cong \sum_{i=1}^{n} s_i(\mathbf{p_0},\mathbf{w_0},\mathbf{z_0}) \;\; p_i \;+\; \frac{1}{2}\sum_{i=1}^{n}\sum_{j=1}^{n} \frac{\partial s_i(\mathbf{p_0},\mathbf{w_0},\mathbf{z_0})}{\partial p_i} \; \Delta p_i \; \Delta p_j, \tag{19}$$

where $s_i(\mathbf{p_0},\mathbf{w},\mathbf{z})$ is the supply of good i given the original price vector $\mathbf{p_0}$. This is the expression used to calculate nominal income in VASEM (see equations 3 and 4 in Appendix 4).

A simplified version of this equation is used to calculate the household-level impact of rice price changes. Because the calculations are limited to the impact of a single producer price (that of rice) on farm income, the product subscripts are dropped. The partial in the second term is converted into a supply price elasticity (ε_{ij}^{S}):

$$\Delta x \cong s_r(\mathbf{p_0},\mathbf{w_0},\mathbf{z_0}) \;\; p_r \;+\; \frac{1}{2}\, \varepsilon_{rr}^{S} \frac{s_r(\mathbf{p_0},\mathbf{w_0},\mathbf{z_0})}{p_{0r}} \; \Delta p_r \; \Delta p_r, \tag{20}$$

where s_r and p_r refer to the supply and price of rice, respectively, and the elasticity ε_{rr}^{S} is the own-price elasticity of rice supply. After dividing both sides by the original income (x_0) and multiplying the top and bottom of the right side by p_{0r}, the result is

$$\frac{\Delta x}{x_0} \cong \frac{p_{0r}\, s_r(\mathbf{p_0},\mathbf{w_0},\mathbf{z_0})}{x_0} \; \frac{\Delta p_r}{p_{0r}} + \frac{1}{2}\varepsilon_{rr}^{S} \; \frac{p_{0r}\, s_r(\mathbf{p_0},\mathbf{w_0},\mathbf{z_0})}{x_{0r}} \left(\frac{\Delta p_r}{p_{0r}} \right)^2 . \tag{21}$$

Finally, PR_r, the production ratio for rice, is defined as the value of rice production as a proportion of income (or total expenditure):

$$\frac{x}{x_0} \cong PR_r \; \frac{p_r}{p_{0r}} + \frac{1}{2}\varepsilon_{rr}^{S} \; PR_r \left(\frac{p_r}{p_{0r}^{p}} \right)^2 . \tag{22}$$

Combining equations (16) (the impact of retail price changes on consuming households) and equation (22) (the effect of producer price changes on farm households), the following expression is obtained:

$$\frac{\Delta w^2}{x_0} \cong \frac{\Delta p_r^{p}}{p_{0r}^{p}} \; PR_r + \frac{1}{2}\left(\frac{\Delta p_r^{p}}{p_{0r}^{p}} \right)^2 PR_r \; \varepsilon_{rr}^{S} - \frac{\Delta p_r^{c}}{p_{0r}^{c}} \; CR_r - \frac{1}{2}\left(\frac{\Delta p_r^{p}}{p_{0r}^{p}} \right)^2 CR_r \; \varepsilon_{rr}^{H} , \tag{23}$$

where Δw^2 ($= \Delta x - CV$) is the second-order approximation of the net welfare effect of a rice price change on a household and the superscripts p and c are used to distinguish between the prices used to value rice production and consumption, respectively.

This expression incorporates the response of consumers and producers to the price change. The immediate welfare impact of the price change is obtained by setting the elasticities equal to zero:

$$\frac{\Delta w^1}{x_0} = \frac{\Delta p_r^p}{p_{0r}^p} PR_r - \frac{\Delta p_r^c}{p_{0r}^c} CR_r , \tag{24}$$

where Δw^1 is the first-order approximation of the net welfare effect of a price change.

APPENDIX 3

Foreign Demand Elasticity for Vietnamese Rice

The price elasticity of export demand is the percentage change in export demand facing a country given a 1 percent change in its export price, taking into account the response of both importers and other exporters. This is equivalent to the change in a country's exports necessary to cause a 1 percent change in world price. The "small-country assumption" is that the level of exports (or imports) does not affect the price it receives, implying that the elasticity of export demand is minus infinity.

One method of obtaining export demand elasticities is to estimate them econometrically with time-series data by regressing export demand on the export price and other variables. This approach has a number of methodological problems including measurement error (the prices may vary due to changes in quality), endogeneity (the volume of exports affects export prices), and omitted variables. It is argued that these errors tend to bias the estimated elasticities toward zero (Tyers and Anderson 1988).

A second method is to calculate the export demand elasticity using information from all other countries on supply and demand elasticities, production and consumption volumes, and elasticities of price transmission. This type of analysis is usually carried out using a model of world agricultural trade. The elasticity of export demand for a reference country (ε_{xr}) can be expressed in terms of the elasticity of net import demand by all other countries (ε_{mi}):

$$\varepsilon_{xr} = \frac{\partial X_r P_r}{\partial P_r X_r} = \frac{P_r}{X_r} \sum_{i \neq r} \frac{\partial M_i \, \partial P_i}{\partial P_i \, \partial P_r} = \frac{P_r}{X_r} \sum_{i \neq r} \varepsilon_{mi} \frac{M_i}{P_i} \theta_{ir} \frac{P_i}{P_r} = \sum_{i \neq r} \varepsilon_{mi} \theta_{ir} \frac{M_i}{X_r}, \qquad (25)$$

where X_r is exports from the reference country, M_i is net imports by country i ($i \neq r$), P is price, and θ_{ir} is the elasticity of prices in country i with respect to the price in the reference country. The elasticity of net import demand for country i (ε_{mi}) can be expressed in terms of domestic supply and demand elasticities (ε_S and ε_D, respectively).

$$\varepsilon_{Mi} = \frac{\partial M_i \, \partial P_i}{\partial P_i \, \partial M_i} = \left(\frac{\partial D_i}{\partial P_i} - \frac{\partial S_i}{\partial P_i} \right) \frac{P_i}{M_i} = \left(\varepsilon_{Di} \frac{D_i}{P_i} - \varepsilon_{Si} \frac{S_i}{P_i} \right) \frac{P_i}{M_i} = \varepsilon_{Di} \frac{D_i}{M_i} - \varepsilon_{Si} \frac{S_i}{M_i} . \tag{26}$$

Combining these two equations gives

$$\varepsilon_{xr} = \sum_{i \neq r} \left(\varepsilon_{Di} \frac{D_i}{M_i} - \varepsilon_{Si} \frac{S_i}{M_i} \right) \theta_{ir} \frac{M_i}{X_r} = \sum_{i \neq r} \left(\varepsilon_{Di} \frac{D_i}{X_r} - \varepsilon_{Si} \frac{S_i}{X_r} \right) \theta_{ir} . \tag{27}$$

Other things being equal, the export demand will be more elastic when (1) exports from the reference country are small relative to world production, (2) the supply and demand elasticities in importing and exporting countries are large in absolute value, and (3) the elasticity of price transmission is high.

Two econometric studies of the export demand for Thai rice have been carried out. Using data from the 1950s and 1960s, Tsujii (1973) estimated the export demand elasticity for Thailand to be near unity. Wong (1978), using more recent data, estimated the short-run price elasticity of export demand for Thai rice at –4.0. The World Bank (1983) endorsed this estimate, stating that the long-run elasticity would be in the neighborhood of –10.

A number of multiregional models of world agricultural trade have been developed. One of the most comprehensive models is the Grains, Livestock, and Sugar (GLS) model developed by Tyers and Anderson (1988). It includes seven commodity groups and 30 countries/regions and uses a dynamic structure allowing it to forecast short- and long-run effects of policy intervention. According to this model, the export demand elasticity for Thai rice is –8.3 in the short run and –17.3 in the long run.

The export demand elasticity for Vietnamese rice can be approximated by adjusting the Thai elasticities, using the ratio of world production to country exports. In 1980–82 (the reference years for the GLS model), world rice production (264 million tons) was 85 times larger than Thai exports (3.1 million tons). In 1995, world production (371 million tons) was 148 times larger than Vietnamese exports. If the elasticities of supply, demand, and price transmission are assumed to be constant, the export demand elasticity for Vietnamese rice in 1995 would be 1.74 times larger than the elasticity for Thai rice in 1980–82. Using the results of Tyers and Anderson (1992), this would imply elasticities of export demand for Vietnamese rice to be –14.4 in the short run and –30.1 in the long run. Given the trend toward reducing trade barriers, including the relaxation of rice self-sufficiency policies in Indonesia, it is likely that the price transmission elasticity has increased since 1980–82. Thus, –15 and –30 are adopted here as the short- and long-run elasticities of export demand for Vietnamese rice.

APPENDIX 4

Description of the Viet Nam Agricultural Spatial Equilibrium Model

The Viet Nam Agricultural Spatial Equilibrium Model (VASEM) consists of 12 blocks of equations and 12 sets of endogenous variables (see the list below). The model is written in the General Algebraic Modeling System (GAMS), using the mixed complementarity programming (MCP) solver (Brooke, Kendrick, and Meeraus 1992). MCP is an algorithm for finding the values of the endogenous variables that satisfy a set of equations and inequalities (Rutherford 1995).

The supply of each commodity in each region is a function of the four commodity prices in that region (equation 1). For simplicity, a log-linear specification of supply is used. The own-price elasticities are derived from a time-series analysis of supply response in Viet Nam (Khiem and Pingali 1996). The cross-price elasticities are derived under the assumption that half of the area taken in (out) of a given crop is reallocated proportionately to the other three crops.

Demand (equation 2) is specified using the linear approximation of the Almost Ideal Demand System (Deaton and Muelbauer 1980). The income and price elasticities were estimated using household data from the Viet Nam Living Standards Survey (VLSS)(GSO 1994; World Bank 1995b).

Nominal per capita income (equation 3) is calculated as the sum of the original income plus a second-order (trapezoidal) approximation of the producer surplus resulting from the change in prices. Real per capita income (equation 4) is nominal per capita income minus a second-order approximation of the consumer surplus associated with the price changes.

The price used for valuing output (equation 5) is a weighted average of consumer and farm gate prices, where the weights are the regional share of output sold and consumed at home, respectively.[37]

[37] This approach was adopted for two reasons. First, it is consistent with the valuation of agricultural production in the VLSS, which was the source of the income data in the model. Second, this method reflects the fact that for commercial rice growers, the opportunity cost of rice production is the producer price, while for the 51 percent of rural households that are net rice buyers, the opportunity cost is the consumer price.

Since Viet Nam now accounts for 10 to 12 percent of world rice exports, it is preferable to treat it as a "large country" in international rice markets. World rice prices are made a function of Vietnamese rice exports and the price elasticity of world demand for Vietnamese rice is –15 in the short run and –30 in the long run (equation 6).

Three inequalities define the spatial relationships among prices. One (equation 7) ensures that domestic price differentials do not exceed the larger of (1) the estimated cost of transportation between the regions and (2) the price differentials observed in 1995. The other two inequalities (equations 8 and 9) keep domestic prices below the import parity price and above the export parity price, respectively, for each crop in each region.

Two inequalities maintain the commodity balance in each region, one connecting supply and outflows (equation 10) and the other connecting demand and inflows (equation 11). And one inequality keeps rice exports less than or equal to the rice export quota (equation 12).

Label	Equation	Number in model
1	Supply	28
2	Demand	28
3	Nominal per capita income	7
4	Real per capita income	7
5	Price for valuing output	28
6	World demand for rice	1
7	Inflows	28
8	Outflows	28
9	Domestic price relations	196
10	Import-domestic price relations	28
11	Export-domestic price relations	28
12	Export quota	4
		411

Symbol	Endogenous variable	Number in model
BS_{cr}	Budget share for commodity c in region r	28
S_{cr}	Supply of commodity c in region r	28
PS_{cr}	Producer price for commodity c in region r	28
PP_{cr}	Price for valuing output of commodity c in region r	28
PD_{cr}	Consumer price for commodity c in region r	28
M_{cr}	Imports of commodity c into region r	28
X_{cr}	Export of commodity c from region r	28
PX_{rice}	Export (f.o.b.) price of rice	1
$TQ_{crr'}$	Quantities of commodity c transported from region r to region r'	196
Y_r	Nominal per capita income in region r	7
YR_r	Real per capita income in region r	7
IXT_c	Implicit export tax associated with quota	4
		411

Symbol	Parameter
α_{cr}^{S}	Constant in the supply equation of crop *c* in region *r*
$\beta_{cc'r}^{S}$	Coefficient for the effect of the price of crop *c'* on the supply of crop *c* in region *r*
α_{cr}^{D}	Constant in the demand equation for crop *c* in region *r*
$\beta_{cc'r}^{D}$	Coefficient for the effect of the price of commodity *c'* on the demand for commodity *c* in region *r*
θ_{cr}	Coefficient for the effect of income on the demand for commodity *c* in region *r*
Y_r^0	Original per capita income in region *r*
PP_{cr}^{0}	Original price for valuing output of commodity *c* in region *r*
ω_{cr}	Share of output sold for commodity *c* in region *r*
$SS_{cc'r}$	Partial derivative of the supply of commodity *c* with respect to the price of commodity *c'* in region *r*
α^W	Constant in the world demand for Vietnamese rice
β^W	Price coefficient of the world demand for Vietnamese rice
POP_r	Population of region *r*
$TP_{rr'}$	Transportation costs from region *r* to region *r'*
$ITX_{crr'}$	Implicit tax on internal transportation of commodity *c* from region *r* to region *r'*
PM_c	Import (c.i.f.) price of commodity *c*
PX_c	Export (f.o.b.) price of commodity *c* (PX_{rice} is an endogenous variable)
$QUOTA_c$	Export quota on crop *c*

1. Supply:

$$\ln(S_{cr}) = \alpha_{cr}^{s} + \sum_{c'=1}^{4} \beta_{cc'r}^{s} \ln(PS_{c'r}).$$

2. Demand

$$BS_{cr} = \alpha_{cr}^{D} + \sum_{c'=1}^{4} \beta_{cc'r}^{D} \ln(PD_{c'r}) + \theta_{cr} \ln\left|YR_r\right|.$$

3. Nominal per capita income

$$Y_r = Y_r^0 + \sum_{c=1}^{4} S_{cr}^{0}(PP_{cr} - PP_{cr}^{0}) \;/\; POP_r$$
$$+ \frac{1}{2} \sum_{c=1}^{4} \sum_{c'=1}^{4} (PP_{cr} - PP_{cr}^{0}) SS_{cc'r} (PP_{c'r} - PP_{c'r}^{0}) \;/\; POP_r$$

4. Real per capita income

$$YR_r = Y_r^0 + \sum_{c=1}^{4} S_{cr}^0 (PP_{cr} - PP_{cr}^0) \,/\, POP_r$$
$$+ \frac{1}{2} \sum_{c=1}^{4} \sum_{c'=1}^{4} (PP_{cr} - PP_{cr}^0) SS_{cc'r} (PP_{c'r} - PP_{c'r}^0) \quad / \, POP_r$$
$$- \sum_{c=1}^{4} D_{cr}^0 (PD_{cr} - PD_{cr}^0) \,/\, POP_r$$
$$- \frac{1}{2} \sum_{c=1}^{4} \sum_{c'=1}^{4} (PD_{cr} - PD_{cr}^0) DS_{cc'r} (PD_{c'r} - PD_{c'r}^0) \quad / \, POP_r$$

5. Price for valuing output

$$PP_{cr} = \omega_{cr} \, PS_{cr} + (1 - \omega_{cr}) \, PS_{cr}.$$

6. World demand for Vietnamese rice

$$\sum_{r=1}^{7} X_{rice,r} = \alpha^w + \beta^w \, PX_{rice}.$$

7. Outflows

$$S_{cr} \geq \sum_{r'=1}^{7} TQ_{crr'} + X_{cr}.$$

8. Inflows

$$\sum_{r'=1}^{7} TQ_{cr'r} + M_{cr} \geq \left(\frac{BS_{cr} \, Y_r}{PD_{cr}} \right) POP_r.$$

9. Domestic price relations

$$PS_{cr} + TP_{rr'} + ITX_{rr'} + MKT_c \geq PD_{cr'}.$$

10. Import-domestic price relations

$$PM_c + TP_{world\,r} + ITX_{world\,r} \geq PD_{cr}.$$

11. Export-domestic price relations

$$PS_{cr} + TP_{world\,r} + ITX_{rworld} + ITX_{c} \geq PX_{c}.$$

12. Export quota

$$\sum_{r=1}^{7} X_{cr} \leq QUOTA_{c}.$$

References

Akaike, H. 1969. Fitting autoregressive models for prediction. *Annals of the Institute of Statistical Mathematics* 21 (2): 243–248.

Anderson, K. 1998. *Vietnam's transforming economy and WTO accession.* Centre for International Economic Studies. Adelaide: University of Adelaide.

Arraudeau, M. A., and V-T. Xuan. 1995. Opportunities for upland rice research in Vietnam. In *Vietnam and IRRI: A partnership in rice research,* ed. G. L. Denning and V-T. Xuan. Manila: International Rice Research Institute and the Ministry of Agriculture and Food Industry.

Barrett, C. B., and P. A. Dorosh. 1996. Farmers' welfare and changing food prices: Nonparametric evidence from rice in Madagascar. *American Journal of Agricultural Economics* 78 (August): 656–669.

Baulch, B. 1997. Transfer costs, spatial arbitrage, and testing for food market integration. *American Journal of Agricultural Economics* 79 (2): 477–487.

Blyn, G. 1973. Price series correlation as a measure of market integration. *Indian Journal of Agricultural Economics* 71: 661–669.

Bourguignon, F., J. de Melo, and C. Morrisson. 1991. Poverty and income distribution during adjustment: Issues and evidence from the OECD project. *World Development* 19 (11): 1485–1508.

Bray, F. 1986. *The rice economies: Technology and development in Asian societies.* Oxford, U.K.: Basil Blackwell.

Brooke, A., D. Kendrick, and A. Meeraus. 1992. *GAMS: A user's guide, Release 2.25.* Danvers, Mass., U.S.A.: Boyd and Fraser.

Budd, J. W. 1993. Changing food prices and rural welfare: A nonparametric examination of the Côte d'Ivoire. *Economic Development and Cultural Change* 41 (April): 587–603.

CIE (Center for International Economics). 1998. Vietnam's trade policies. Paper prepared for the World Bank. CIE, Canberra.

———. 1999. Non-tariff barriers in Vietnam: A framework for developing a phase-out strategy. Paper prepared for the World Bank. CIE, Canberra.

Cornia, G., R. Jolly, and R. Jolly, eds. 1987. *Adjustment with a human face: Protecting the vulnerable and promoting growth.* Oxford: Clarendon.

Cosslett, T. L., and W. R. Shaw. 1987. Economy. In *Vietnam: A country study,* ed. R. J. Cima. Washington, D.C.: Department of the Army.

Dac, N. T. 1996. Economic analysis of rice production in the Red River Delta of Viet Nam. M.Sc. thesis, Chiang Mai University, Chiang Mai, Thailand.

Dao, H.G. 1999. Identification of WTO inconsistent policies. Paper presented at a conference on competitiveness in Viet Nam, sponsored by the Japanese International Cooperation Agency, Hanoi, July 1999.

Deaton, A. 1989. Rice prices and income distribution in Thailand: A non-parametric analysis. *Economic Journal* 99 (395) (Supplement): 1–37.

Deaton, A., and J. Muelbauer. 1980. An almost ideal demand system. *American Economic Review* 70 (3): 312–326.

Dien, L. D. 1995. Postharvest technology for food grains in Vietnam. In *Postharvest technology for agricultural products in Vietnam*, ed. B. R. Champ and E. Highley. Proceedings of an international workshop, held in Hanoi, Viet Nam, December 1994. Canberra: Australian Centre for International Agricultural Research.

Dorosh, P., and S. Haggblade. 1993. Agriculture-led growth: Foodgrains versus export crops in Madagascar. *Agricultural Economics* 9 (2): 165–180.

Dung, N. H. 1994. Profitability and price response of rice production systems in the Mekong River Delta, Vietnam. M.Sc. thesis, Chiang Mai University, Chiang Mai, Thailand.

Engle, R. F., and C. W. J. Granger. 1987. Cointegration and error correction: Representation, estimation, and testing. *Econometrica* 55 (2): 251–276.

Farruk, M. O. 1970. *The structure and performance of the marketing system in East Pakistan.* Occasional Paper 31. Ithaca, N.Y.: Cornell University, Department of Agricultural Economics.

FAO (Food and Agriculture Organization of the United Nations). 1998. *FAO fertilizer yearbook 1997.* Rome.

———. Various years. FAOSTAT database <http://apps.fao.org>.

Foster, J., J. Greer, and E. Thorbecke. 1984. A class of decomposable poverty measures. *Econometrica* 52 (3): 761–66.

Goletti, F. 1994. *The changing public role in a rice economy approaching self-sufficiency: The case of Bangladesh.* Research Report 98. Washington, D.C.: International Food Policy Research Institute.

GSO (General Statistical Office). 1994. *Viet Nam living standards survey 1992–93.* Hanoi: Statistical Publishing House.

———. 1995a. *Statistical yearbook 1994.* Hanoi: Statistical Publishing House.

———. 1995b. *Ket qua tong dieu tra nong thon va nong nghiep nam* [Results of the agricultural census of 1994]. 3 vols. Hanoi: Statistical Publishing House.

———. 1996a. *Statistical yearbook 1995.* Hanoi: Statistical Publishing House.

———. 1996b. *Viet Nam 1985–1995: Statistical data of agriculture, forestry, and fishery.* Hanoi: Statistical Publishing House.

———. 1999. *Viet Nam living standards survey 1997–98.* Hanoi: Statistical Publishing House.

Harriss, B. 1979. There is a method in my madness: Or is it vice-versa? Measuring agricultural product performance. *Food Research Institute Studies* 17 (2): 197–218.

Huang, J., and C. David. 1993. Demand for cereal grains in Asia: The effect of urbanization. *Agricultural Economics* 8 (2): 107–124.

Huang, J., C. David, and B. Duff. 1991. Rice in Asia: Is it becoming an inferior good? Comment. *American Journal of Agricultural Economics* 73 (2): 515–521.

IFPRI (International Food Policy Research Institute). 1996. Rice market monitoring and policy options study. Final report submitted to the Asian Development Bank under Project No. TA 2224-VIE. Washington, D.C.

IRRI (International Rice Research Institute). 1991. *World rice statistics 1990.* Los Banos, Philippines.

Ito, S., E. W. F. Peterson, and W. R. Grant. 1989. Rice in Asia: Is it becoming an inferior good? *American Journal of Agricultural Economics* 71 (1): 32–42.

Jones, W. O. 1972. *Marketing staple food crops in tropical Africa.* Ithaca, N.Y.: Cornell University Press.

Khiem, N. T., and P. L. Pingali. 1995. Supply response of rice and three food crops in Vietnam. In *Vietnam and IRRI: A partnership in rice research*, ed. G. L. Denning and V-T. Xuan. Manila: International Rice Research Institute and the Ministry of Agriculture and Food Industry.

Kim, T. H. 1996. *Vietnam's economy: The period 1945–1995 and its perspectives by the year 2020.* Hanoi: Statistical Publishing House.

Kreamer, R. 2000. Personal communication from the agricultural attaché, Foreign Agricultural Service, U.S. Department of Agriculture, Hanoi, January 24.

Krishnaiah, J. 1995. Spatial equilibrium models in agricultural marketing research: A simplified exposition. In *Prices, products, and people*, ed. G. Scott. Boulder, Colo., U.S.A.: Lynne Reinner

Lele, U. 1972. *Food marketing in India: Private performance and public policy.* Ithaca, N.Y., U.S.A.: Cornell University Press.

Mellor, J. 1978. Food price policy and income distribution in low-income countries. *Economic Development and Cultural Change* 27 (1): 1–26.

Minot, N. 1998. Mapping poverty and agro-ecological potential in Viet Nam. Paper prepared for the United Nations Development Program project on Strengthening Capacity for the Renewal of Rural Development in Viet Nam, Phase I. International Food Policy Research Institute, Washington, D.C.

———. 2000. Generating disaggregated poverty maps: An application to Vietnam. *World Development* 28 (2): 319–331.

Nguyen, T. N. 1999. Producing and life status of landless and lack of land households in the Mekong Delta River. Paper presented at a conference on competitiveness in Viet Nam, sponsored by the Japanese International Cooperation Agency, Hanoi, July 1999.

O'Mara, G., and L-S. Vinh. 1985. *The supply and welfare effects of rice-pricing policies in Thailand.* Staff Working Paper No. 714. Washington, D.C.: World Bank.

Pingali, P. L., and V-T. Xuan. 1992. Vietnam: Decollectivization and rice productivity growth. *Economic Development and Cultural Change* 40 (4): 697–718.

Pingali, P. L., M. Hossain, and R. V. Gerpacio. 1997. *Asian rice bowls: The returning crisis?* Oxon, U.K.: CAB International for the International Rice Research Institute.

Pingali, P. L., V-T. Xuan, N. T. Khiem, and R. V. Gerpacio. 1998. Prospects for sustaining Vietnam's re-acquired rice exporter status. *Food Policy* 22 (4): 345–358.

Ravallion, M. 1986. Testing market integration. *American Journal of Agricultural Economics* 68 (1): 102–109.

Rutherford, T. 1995. Extension of GAMS for complementarity problems arising in applied economic analysis. *Journal of Economic Dynamics and Control* 19 (8): 1299–1324.

Sahn, D. 1988. The effect of price and income changes on food-energy intake in Sri Lanka. *Economic Development and Cultural Change* 36 (2): 314–340.

Sicular, T. 1989. *Food price policies in Asia.* Ithaca, N.Y.: Cornell University Press.

Sub-NIAPP (Sub-National Institute for Agricultural Planning and Projection). 1995. *Processing, marketing, and consuming rice in the Mekong River Delta.* Ho Chi Minh City.

Takayama, T., and G. G. Judge. 1964. Spatial equilibrium and quadratic programming. *Journal of Farm Economics* 46 (1): 67–93.

Timmer, P. C. 1974. A model of rice marketing margins in Indonesia. *Food Research Institute Studies* 13 (2): 145–167.

Trairatvorakul, P. 1984. *The effects on income distribution and nutrition of alternative rice price policies in Thailand.* Research Report 46. Washington, D.C.: International Food Policy Research Institute.

Tsujii, H. 1973. An econometric study of the effects of national rice policies and the

Green Revolution on national rice economies and international rice trade among less developed countries: With special reference to Thailand, Indonesia, Japan, and the U.S. Ph.D. dissertation, University of Illinois. Cited in Panayotou, T. 1989. Thailand: The experience of a food exporter. In *Food price policy in Asia: A comparative study*, ed. T. Sicular. Ithaca, N.Y., U.S.A.: Cornell University Press.

Tyers, R., and K. Anderson. 1988. Imperfect price transmission and implied trade elasticities in a multicommodity world. In *Elasticities in international agricultural trade,* ed. C. A. Carter and W. H. Gardiner. Boulder, Colo.: Westview Press.

———. 1992. *Disarray in world food markets: A quantitative assessment.* Cambridge and New New York: Cambridge University Press.

U.S. Department of Agriculture. 1995. Evolving grain markets in Southeast Asia. *Grains: World markets and trade* (June).

Vien, N. K. 1993. *Vietnam: A long history.* Hanoi: Gioi Publishers.

Warr, P. G. 1997. *General equilibrium welfare and distributional effects of Thailand's rice export tax.* Working Papers in Trade and Development No. 97/1. Canberra: Australia National University.

Weber, M. T., J. M. Staatz, J. S. Holtzman, E. W. Crawford, and R.H. Bernsten. 1988. Informing food security decisions in Africa: Empirical analysis and policy dialogue. *American Journal of Agricultural Economics* 70 (5): 1044–1052.

Wong, C. M. 1978. A model for evaluating the effects of Thai government taxation of rice exports on trade and welfare. *American Journal of Agricultural Economics* 60 (1): 65–73.

World Bank. 1995. *Viet Nam: Poverty assessment and strategy.* Washington, D.C.: World Bank.

———. 1996a. *World development report 1996: From plan to market.* New York: Oxford University Pres

———. 1996b. *Vietnam water resources sector review: Main report.* Joint report by the World Bank, Asian Development Bank, Food and Agriculture Organization of the United Nations, United Nations Development Programme, and the NGO Water Resources Group, in cooperation with the Institute of Water Resources Planning (Viet Nam). Washington, D.C.: World Bank.

———. 1997. *World development report 1997: The state in a changing world.* New York: Oxford University Press.

Xuan, V-T. 1995. Rice production, agricultural research, and the environment. In *Vietnam's rural transformation*, ed. B. J. Tria Kerkvliet and D. J. Porter. Boulder, Colo., U.S.A.: Westview Press.

———. 1997. Sustaining diversification in rice areas. Paper presented at the "Workshop on Agriculture and Rural Development Strategy for Viet Nam," cosponsored by Viet Nam, Ministry of Agriculture and Rural Development, the Food and Agriculture Organization of the United Nations, and the World Bank, Hanoi, March.

Xuan, V-T., K. T. Duong, N. N. De, B. C. Buu, P. T. Phan, and D. W. Puckridge. 1995. Deepwater rice research in the Mekong River Delta. In *Vietnam and IRRI: A partnership in rice research,* ed. G. L. Denning and V-T. Xuan. Manila: International Rice Research Institute and the Ministry of Agriculture and Food Industry, the Philippines.

Nicholas Minot is a research fellow and Francesco Goletti is a senior research fellow in the Markets and Structural Studies Division of the International Food Policy Research Institute.

Made in United States
Orlando, FL
17 June 2026

82973232R00072